IN THE TIRE INDUSTRY

When Doing the Same Things Do Not Produce Different Results …

Roger McManus

ENTREPRENEURIAL INSANITY
IN THE TIRE INDUSTRY
When Doing the Same Things Do Not
Produce Different Results ...

Copyright © 2011 by Ensanity Press

Printed in USA   3.2

Dedication

This book is dedicated to my many teachers. I have met you in classrooms, seminars, books and tapes. I have experienced you in success and failure; victories and disappointments. I have collected your wisdom, tested your lessons, enjoyed your approval and suffered your reproach. I seek only to be worthy of passing on your wisdom through my interpretation of your lessons.

This book is also dedicated to my greatest "tire teacher" Wayne Croswell, past president of the Tire Industry Association who took me under his wing and introduced me to so many people that have helped make this book possible. Through Wayne's introduction, those industry luminaries, who appear in the Acknowledgement pages of this book, have become my advisors, consultants and friends.

And, not ever to be forgotten when you look at how it all gets put together is my most patient and consistent teacher, advisor, consultant and friend, my wife, Patsy.

Roger McManus

Acknowledgements

A book of this type would not be possible without the contributions of many people who have devoted their lives to the tire industry. I am but a visitor, blending a lifetime of my entrepreneurial experience into the tremendous knowledge of those who contributed to this work. The result is a credible strategy for those who own a tire business who want to move from being owners of a small business to owning a growing, entrepreneurial enterprise.

So important are the contributions of those who have given of their time and experience, the following pages will introduce you to them, if it is possible you do not already know them.

I extend my sincerest thanks to each of them for their patience with my naïve questions and constant requests for them to check my work. This book would not be possible without them.

And, thanks to Erik Croswell, for remembering to put me in touch with his Dad after our chance meeting on an airplane that day that now seems so long ago.

THE AUTHOR

Roger McManus

 For well over 30 years, **Roger McManus** has coached, funded, counseled and published for entrepreneurs. As a serial entrepreneur himself, he has garnered the wisdom of dozens of advisers and gathered years of experiences in his effort to develop a clear picture of the entrepreneurial mindset.

In this undertaking, Roger has dived deeply into the tire industry and garnered the cooperation of some of its greatest players. The result is a book that promises to offer those in the tire business a new look at what is probably a very established business.

As a magazine publisher, speaker, author and consultant, McManus has had the rare opportunity to see inside businesses resulting in the conclusion that many call themselves entrepreneurs, but few truly achieve the levels of freedom that the title should imply.

Recognized by the SBA as Media Advocate of the Year and elected to the White House Conference on Small Business, McManus takes the plight and the opportunities of the small business owner to heart in his writing. The *Entrepreneurial Insanity* series explores how changing the point of view, plus the development of a few systems can deliver the objective of business ownership; freedom for the owner to work less in the business while deriving greater value from it.

THE CONTRIBUTORS

Wayne Croswell

Wayne Croswell is president of WECnology, LLC a complimentary advisor for independent tire dealers. For over 30 years he's been designing, developing and providing technology solutions for the auto-motive aftermarket.

Wayne has met with thousands of tire dealers throughout the world, including retail, wholesale, commercial and retread shops. He has served on the TIA Board of Directors since its inception and has served on its Executive Committee as TIA Secretary, Vice President and was its President in 2009-10. He earned his BS degree in Computer Science from Boston College.

Charlie Creighton

Charlie Creighton is the CEO of Colony Tire Corp., one of the country's largest regional dealerships. He was selected *Modern Tire Dealer* magazine's 2007 Tire Dealer of the Year.

Charlie started in 1976 with just two gasoline pumps and added a small oil company in Edenton later that year. In 1979, Charlie purchased a small oil company in Roper, NC and became a Farm Bureau tire dealer there. He began selling Goodyear tires in 1980. Today, his Colony Tire is one of the leading tire distributors in North America with over 550 associates, operating 200 vehicles with 46 locations in NC and Virginia.

Jody DeVere

Jody DeVere, is founder and CEO of AskPatty.com, a marketing-to-women expert, journalist, car care and safety spokesperson.

Jody is currently the COO of the Woman's Automotive Association International, member of the Car Care Council Women's Board, Board Member of the Collision Industry Foundation, member of the SEMA Businesswomen's Networking Association and a Contributing Editor on Blogher.com. Jody continues to do speaking engagements on the auto-motive industry, social media, marketing to women, and everything in between.

Pam Gatto

Pam Gatto followed the footsteps of many in the tire business going to work with her father. Being a woman and dramatically successful – and involved – makes her an exceptional leader in the tire industry.

Pam joined her father, Mike, in 1973. In 1994 Pam assumed the presidency of Gatto's Tires and Auto Service with six retail stores and one commercial location. She served as TIA president and was inducted into the TIA Hall of Fame having achieved both positions in Florida, too. Pam has chaired and served on numerous boards and committees in Brevard County Florida and was selected Entrepreneur of the Year in 2010.

Roy Littlefield

Dr. Roy Littlefield, Executive Vice President of the Tire Industry Association (TIA), has extensive experience in association management including NTDRA and ITRA.

After four years of Capitol Hill experience on the staff of Sen. Thomas McIntyre (D-NH), Roy joined NTDRA as Director of Government Affairs. He continues today as one of the lobbyists for the Tire Industry Association. He holds a BA in History and Politics from Dickinson College and a Master's Degree and Ph.D. (Summa Cum Laude) from Catholic University where he continues to serve as adjunct professor of Politics and American History.

Larry Morgan

Larry Morgan pioneered one of the classic "roll-up" strategies in the tire industry building and accumulating tire businesses until the number exceeded 600.

Larry was named Tire Dealer of the Year in 2001, served as TIA president in 2004 and was inducted into the TIA Hall of Fame in 2008. Wanting to pursue broader interests, today Morgan, with his son Brett, operates nine new car dealerships covering 10 different brands. He is a principal or director in nearly a dozen additional businesses. He has been named TIME magazine Dealer of the Year in Florida along with dozens of other accolades acknowledging his entrepreneurial leadership.

Table of Contents

INTRODUCTION

From Insanity to Independence

This book is the product of experience, much of it my own. They say that experience is the best teacher. I am well educated.

This book is the product of observation. I have had the good fortune to work with hundreds of different business owners. I observed the patterns. To accomplish this book I solicited, and gracefully received, the observations of many people whose lives are centered in the tire industry.

This book is the product of disappointment. I have personally experienced and also observed the bright dreams of would-be entrepreneurs who remained small business owners who never stopped owning a job instead of an asset.

This book is the product of inspiration. It came about as a result of one of those "Aha!" moments when all that I had experienced academically came rushing forward to become reality. That "Aha!" can be summed up in a single statement: ***Those who start businesses rarely think of their venture as an investment; they just want to own something that will provide them with a job.***

This book is the product of accumulation. Over the years, as I have published magazines for small business owners, been involved with trade organizations large and small and

13

consulted with larger corporations, I have accumulated the experiences and the stories that made the first book *Entrepreneurial Insanity*, possible. *Entrepreneurial Insanity in the Tire Industry* combines my own experiences with those of much greater depth and tenure. The blend of experiences results in powerful guidance for you.

This book is the product of an Objective. If this book does its job, it will move you, the owner of a small tire business into an entrepreneur's mindset. Your definition of "tire business" will be altered forever. It will shift your motivation from making a living, to developing an asset. It will move you from the position of being in business to being exactly like the money suppliers you may have approached. Money suppliers, you see, do not care about owning a business; they care about creating a saleable asset – and making a profit.

When the owner of a small business focuses on the goal of establishing the enterprise as a salable entity – whether he or she actually sells it or not – there is a massive shift in intention and attention. From that point, every decision is based on whether it is good for the enterprise as an entity totally separate from the owner.

The metamorphosis from small business owner to entrepreneur is the process of ending the insanity with which so many owners of small businesses suffer today.

This book is the product of "entrepreneurial insanity".

CHAPTER 1

Are You Involved or Insane?

Work harder !
Work smarter, not harder !
Concentrate !
Focus your attention !
Motivate your people !
Plan your day !

Over the years, you have heard them all. And, for football teams and high school students, these admonitions are just fine. But, working, concentrating, focusing, motivating and planning are only useful if they are accomplished in a larger picture.

The larger picture is *The Objective*.

It is the constant attempts to "do better" by working harder that creates the "insanity". Albert Einstein contributed the definition of Insanity that is now so often quoted, or, in the case of this book, paraphrased, ***"Insanity: Doing the same thing over and over again and expecting different results."***

15

How perfectly this defines how most businesses are operated today! Too many small business owners believe the first six lines of this chapter and believe that, as a result, they can succeed – if they just try harder.

The Pennsylvania Dutch phrase, "The hurrier I go, the behinder I get" would seem to apply equally. Working harder – or hurrier – does not achieve The Objective.

The Objective (capitalized because it is the Holy Grail in this text) is as simple as answering the question, "What do you want to get out of this business you have started?" Or, perhaps, "How do you *get out* of this business you find yourself in?"

THE OBJECTIVE

It is not enough to say "make a living" or, more generally, "make money". Money is not The Objective. It is a tool. It is a good measuring tape. But, it is not The Objective.

Ask any truly aware entrepreneur why he or she has his or her own business and the answer always boils down to some variation of the word "freedom". Sure, money buys you freedom, but having money does not make you free. Ask the owner of an amazingly successful retail store who is making money hand-over-fist, but has to be in his store 100 hours a week to make it happen. Money? Yes. Freedom? Hardly! *Freedom* is The Objective.

Conversely, unless the business produces money, freedom is not even possible. So, yes, it is about money, but that is only part of the story. The quest for freedom begins before the business is even open. If the business is already open – as I suspect is the case with most people reading this book – then the quest for freedom starts today.

A larger percentage of today's owners of tire businesses were "born into" their businesses. They are the second generation owners (Gen Two). As a family business there may have been little choice about being in the business. People in that situation were either "needed" in the business so it was a duty or obligation or it was a profitable alternative to "going out and getting a job".

Either way, the quest for freedom is just the same, often stronger. Generation Two always has new ideas that Generation One had no interest or inclination in pursuing. As Generation Two gains more control, new ways of thinking and astounding new technology make whole different ways of thinking and new paths to growth possible.

As you will learn in these pages, the path to freedom is built entirely on growth. Not more sales, though sales are a by-product of growth. But, true growth is not possible if the owner insists of being the best tire buster in the shop!

The path to freedom starts today as you read the first few chapters in this book. It starts as you feel your mind moving from "doing" to "strategizing"; and from "strategizing" to "executing". The execution of the quest for The Objective will deliver to you the benefits that so many people who start (or inherit) businesses really want, but so few achieve. Our work together, as you move through this text, will allow you to achieve The Objective.

A WARNING.

This process may not make you more popular. Some of your loyal employees will not seem so loyal as you make hard decisions, institute new rules and demand account-ability. Others will understand and relish the respon-sibilities with which you (must) now entrust them.

Nevertheless, you will not end up with the same staff as when you start this process. It simply cannot happen unless you are starting from scratch – and, even then, there will be people whom you thought would be a part of your long-term team that will not make it through the process.

Those who make it through the transition will be happier and more productive. Along the way everyone will have acquired a roadmap that gives the employees more autonomy and gives you more freedom.

A Happy Possibility.

This process *will* make you more popular with your family (that is, of course, unless you are Generation Two working side-by-side with Generation One and try to run roughshod over "traditions" without proper respect to the founders who are still active in the business. Then things can get sticky!)

Being in a family relationship is always strained when one member of the family has a "lover". That lover is the business. The impression that your focus is always elsewhere (previously justified because you are working so hard "for the family") is a strain on love relationships and loving involvement with your children. All too often, committed small business owners (who just think they are entrepreneurs) assume that the family "understands". While that may be logically true, it rarely is emotionally.

Perhaps your interest was piqued by my parenthetical statement ("who just think they are entrepreneurs"). In the pages to come, you will become acutely aware of the difference between *owning a business* and being an *entrepreneur*. In fact, the entire first four chapters are devoted to making that difference abundantly clear.

This book is not designed to make you comfortable. It will be most successful if it turns your world upside down. The objective is not to change what you *do*; there are thousands of books that will tell you what to *do*. The objective is not to tell you what to *think*. The objective of this book is to offer you a pattern of thought that is dramatically different than that of 98 percent of small business owners today – and perhaps an even greater percentage of people in the tire business!

There are the obvious examples of small businesses that became massive companies like Big-O, Les Schwab or Discount Tire. And, while no one who picks up this text may own a multi-million dollar corporation as a result, anyone who adjusts their thinking in the way they approach what they are doing will experience a shift in awareness that will yield extremely positive results and, hopefully, achieve The Objective – your freedom from running the business and (finally) experience the joy of owning a business.

CHAPTER 2

Are You a Small Business Owner or an Entrepreneur?

It is fun to call yourself an *entrepreneur*. The French word slips off the tongue and has an elegance about it that sounds so much better than "small business owner". So, without recrimination, many small business owners like to call themselves "entrepreneurs". Owners of tire operations who call themselves "entrepreneurs" are not deluding themselves, they are usually just wrong.

The difference between entrepreneurism and small business ownership is night and day. It is not unlike the difference between a "cook" and a "chef". Truth be known, there are not very many true chefs in the entire world. There are millions of cooks, many of whom *call* themselves "chefs". It is not deceptive. It is just incorrect.

And, the issue is not just one of semantics. The person who considers herself to be a great cook – maybe even a great chef – often thinks that such skill is sufficient to open a restaurant. She knows how to do the preparation; why not create a business around what she loves to do?

The tire store owners who understand tires, under-the-car systems and under-the-hood elements is the perfect candidate for a successful store owner. It just may not be enough to achieve The Objective.

THE DIFFERENCE

The critical difference between being skilled at cooking and being skilled at running a restaurant is dramatic! Knowing the right amount of ingredients in the goulash is very different from balancing inventory and managing vendors, staffing the front and back of the house, grasping all of the various regulatory requirements, making payroll, paying rent, keeping the liquor license, pricing the menus and dancing with the health inspector.

Further, it is very possible that the entrepreneur who owns a successful restaurant doesn't even know how to cook all that well!

The critical difference between being a skilled mechanic and being skilled at running an auto services business is equally dramatic. Knowing how to properly align a steering system is very different from managing payroll and inventory, advertising and bookkeeping, handling hazardous waste correctly and keeping the OSHA inspectors at bay.

And, it is very possible that the entrepreneur who owns a very successful tire operation may not even know how to bust a tire!!

And, even when those skills are acquired, the title "entrepreneur' may not apply. Perhaps "manager" or the term used in this text, "Overseer". Not Entrepreneur.

The title "entrepreneur" is conferred when all of the detail is codified in a series of systems and combined in an *Operations Manual* that is so clear that the owner is not needed at all! He has the freedom to study new profit centers, acquire new locations or create a larger community image by getting involved with the Chamber of Commerce, for example.

Perhaps the easiest way to make the distinction is to use the example of the owner of a hamburger stand – no chefs involved here! The small business owner of a hamburger stand decides that he wants to grow. The quickest and easiest way to grow is to put coupons in the paper and a sign in the window advertising discounted hamburgers (or bigger ones, or tastier ones, or hamburgers made 100 different ways). He uses all of his marketing resources to generate more sales. The entrepreneur, on the other hand, expends his resources in an effort to open more restaurants. He knows the first hamburger stand will operate just fine without him directly involved on a day-to-day basis because he has first established systems that replace him.

It is a matter of scale. It is a matter of mind set. It is the difference between growing sales and growing the business.

The entrepreneur understands that when he grows the business, he is no longer selling hamburgers. He is developing *business systems.* Ultimately, if they are successful, he can sell those business systems, perhaps as a franchise. And, he never loses sight of the fact that he might be selling hamburger restaurant business systems, but he is never selling hamburgers.

It is absolutely the only way an individual can ever open a second location – or 10 more – and survive financially or emotionally.

The hamburger scenario is the key to the ***Entrepreneurial Insanity*** concept. The thesis and focus of this book is that entrepreneurism is a mindset that triggers entirely different behaviors than that typically exhibited by a small business person. The objective is to help the reader redefine entre-preneurism and, as a consequence, take a different path toward small business ownership. If you are reading this book before you open your business, even better. You may be able to jump over a few painful steps

GROWTH

The entrepreneur is defined by a single guiding principal – *growth.* He understands that he has limited personal capacity, no matter how skilled he might be. To grow, he must have people. And, those people will not always be the most brilliant, forward-thinking, goal-minded indi-viduals. If they were, they would have opened their *own* tire businesses! No, the entrepreneur understands that

24

normal people, frankly, _un_exceptional people, will be the backbone of his enterprises. What the entrepreneur brings to the party is a *vision* and a *system*.

That is not to say that the entrepreneur does not seek the help and counsel of talented people. The smartest entrepreneurs hire people more skilled than themselves and have the maturity to *know* what they do not know. But, for the majority of the people who are working in your business on a day-to-day basis, it is folly to think that they are going to be consistently above average, even with the best screening and hiring systems. The most secure way to plan around this probability is to develop business systems that are "ability neutral"; systems that a properly hired and trained individual can execute because they are clear and easy to understand and follow. We will cover this topic extensively in this book.

DIFFERENT SKILLS

By way of further clarifying the difference between the entrepreneur and the small business owner, you need to think about the inherent skill set that an entrepreneur brings to the table. That skill set is distinctly different from someone who is inclined to simply open a business. The entrepreneur is a creator, not a manager. The entrepreneur is happy to (and better off to) create the business, develop it as an organized and profitable entity, sell it and move on. Entrepreneurs who stay on too long find themselves becoming bored with the project – regardless of how successful it is – and actually hampering the business by sticking around. Those who stay too long tend to get fired by their investors.

The Generation Two entrepreneur is no less a creator, even though the business is up and running. Once the Gen Two owner is fully in charge (Gen One has let go of the reins), the creation can take many forms – any of which can lead to The Objective. The Gen Two owner's responsibility is to move the business from a place to work to an asset that can be sold -- whether or not he elects to do so.

Where the entrepreneur successfully stays with the business he started is when he uses his inherent creative skill set to expand the business within the niche in which it was originally built. That is how one tire store becomes a group of stores, adds automotive services, develops wholesale accounts and establishes itself as a *brand* separate from Goodyear, Bridgestone or Michelin.

A great example of this is Colony Tire in tiny Edenton, NC (population 6,000) where Charlie Creighton took a small oil distribution company and added Goodyear tires in 1980. Next Charlie added locations (now 46), a retreading operation and started delivering tires to other dealers under the name Atlantic Tire Distributors (since he was often competing at the retail level in the same town as his wholesale customers). The business expanded internationally as the OTR tire business represented a perfect specialty niche.

Charlie personifies the path from small business owner to entrepreneur. And, in the tradition of many Gen One tire dealers, his son, Scott and son-in-law, Andrew are major parts of the business today.

It should be noted that doing everything in this book will not convert you magically from being a small tire business owner to being Charlie Creighton. It will give you a path to follow that is often taken by entrepreneurs. It is my hope, however, that you will be profoundly impacted by the realization that there is a dramatic difference between running a business (a job) and owning a business (entrepreneurism).

Once that mental conversion has occurred, the path to more businesses becomes possible, because all the new businesses are approached in a much different way than the first. Even if you don't jump on the growth bandwagon, business ownership will become a much more pleasant experience.

Where the small business owner often gets stuck goes back to the reason that he or she opened the business to begin with. Very often the small business owner comes from the corporate environment where there are structures and rules and all sorts of independence-quashing factors they have come to live with and resent. One day the decision to quit is made – or the job is taken away. The "silver lining" in the loss of the job is the new opportunity to throw off the burden of the corporate limitations and seek what is seen as "freedom" to now make all of the decisions.

All too often the new-found "freedom" is the freedom to decide *which* 80 hours to work each week.

JOB MENTALITY

Unfortunately, many new small business owners bring the "job" mentality right into the new business. They know how to do the task and it becomes their "job" to do it. Employees are hired to help them do the job. Growing means doing more of the job. The more of the job that gets done, the more money the small business person makes. And, that works for a while.

Eventually, however, the job that was so unappealing in the corporate environment is twice or three times as large now that it is being done by the owner. There are longer days and fewer days off. Relief comes with the cost of higher payroll and the job is never done as well as when the owner did it himself. All of this freedom becomes a burden. Life is eaten up by the obligation. It stops being fun. Sometimes it becomes terrifying. (See Chapter 7 for more on the topic of Entrepreneurial Terror.)

On the other hand, the entrepreneur works to avoid being caught in this mindset. The small business owner creates his job and gets things done by working hard and hiring help when he needs it. The entrepreneur creates an enterprise that gets things done *through* him, not *by* him. He has the power to create, more than the desire to do. He has a *growth mentality*.

The entrepreneur succeeds or fails based on the strength of ideas and systems. The small business owner succeeds or fails based on the limits of personal stamina. All too often the business kills – spiritually, if not literally – the owner who started it.

Therein lies the invitation to change: to make the move from a position that Michael Gerber described in the *E-Myth* as "working *in* the business" to one of "working *on* the business"; from being a small business owner to becoming an entrepreneur. Therein lies the path to The Objective.

CHAPTER 3

Do You Own an Asset
or a Job You Can't Quit?

REMEMBER HOW IT ALL STARTED?

You have had it with the job – or the job is now gone.
Either way, you have decided to make it on your own. You
are going to start a business. You will be the boss. You
will control your own destiny. You will achieve the
freedom (that word!) that you could never have when
working for someone else. It is a thrilling time!

So you create a place to go to work. You create a *job*.
Your company, Job, Inc., becomes the place you go to do
your work. You go to your *job*.

Even though this is only Chapter 3, you can already sense
the trap, can't you? You have not created a business, you
have created a Job. The Job is what you do. It is what you
know how to do. It is what you do to make money. It may
be very much like the job you left before you created the
new job. Or, it might be very different. But, almost
certainly, it is something you know.

It happens millions of times each year. Displaced or displeased employees become "entrepreneurs" to create a Job to replace their old employment. But, they tell their families, friends and themselves that they are "starting a new business" when, in fact, they are starting a new "Job".

THE DIFFERENCE

What is the difference between owning a business and owning a Job?

The business is a living, breathing thing that the owner creates for the purpose of creating an independent entity that sustains the owner until which time it has matured to the point that it can be sold as a profitable investment.

A Job is an entity created by the owner to make money for himself – and to have something to *do*! It rarely has a plan. It rarely has a defined objective beyond cash flow. It very rarely provides the freedom the creator thought it would. It can rarely be sold for more that the physical assets and salable inventory.

You see it all the time. Ads in *Entrepreneur* magazine are replete with these opportunities to buy a piece of equipment and be in the carpet cleaning *business* or the windshield repair *business* or the locksmith *business*. They are all jobs. Many do not require any labor beyond the owner of the *business*.

Or, the hairstylist who works in someone else's salon gets what Gerber called in *The E-Myth* an "entrepreneurial seizure" and opens her own beauty salon. It is unlikely that this new-born entrepreneur gave a second thought to the distinction between styling hair and running the *business* of styling hair.

Dental schools do a great job of preparing Doctors of Dental Surgery (DDS) to practice densitry. However, they do very little to teach the *business* of dentistry. Think about the range of skills, having nothing to do with dental medicine, that are necessary to establishing a dental practice that is economically viable. Few dentists graduate and open a "store". They join practices with other dentists or they occasionally buy existing practices where the staff teaches the new owner the *business* of dentistry. But, you can see the distinct difference between dentistry and creating a business.

Perhaps the tire business was in the family and your *job* is a foregone conclusion. Eventual ownership is assumed, but moving from *employee* (and bosses son) to *owner* and from owner to *entrepreneur* is the task before you.

Or, maybe you were working for a large company in the tire business and the store you now own was more or less "thrust upon" you by a combination of obligation and opportunity. The transition from the "Big Corporate" environment to being a store owner to becoming a tire industry entrepreneur can be a whole series of challenging phases.

Or, maybe you decided to invest in a tire store on your own. Will it be a job or an asset?

You can see examples in all types of businesses:

- The auto mechanic opens his own tire service. The difference between tire mounting and turnover is significant.

- The baker in the college cafeteria opens her own bakery. The difference between meringue and marketing is huge.

- The band teacher at the local high school opens a musical instrument store. The difference between an intermezzo and inventory management is dramatic.

- The couple that loves to travel and stay in romantic bed and breakfast inns, opens their own. The difference between romance and REVPAR (Revenue Per Available Room) is heartbreaking.

- The regional tire sales manager opens his own tire shop. The difference between filling orders and filling bays is daunting.

The Job vs. The Business of the Job

The Job is not the same as *the business* of performing the Job.

All too often the new business owner takes the work he loves and turns it into a job, all the while thinking he is turning it into a business. This lapse in understanding crushes the spirits of so many that get into business with such high hopes.

The process is predictable. First is the thrill of new business ownership. Next, reality steps in. Then terror, followed by exhaustion and eventually despair.

Why would this be? Because, entrepreneurs do not go into business to get rich; they go into business to gain freedom. And, the freedom does not occur when you have a Job.

This Job is not a good job either. It is a job you cannot quit – your savings and credit are tied up in it. It is a job in which you cannot call in sick because there is no one else to do the job. It is a job you can't sell to someone else – who wants to buy a job? It is a job that eats away at what family life you have, while you hope they understand you are "doing it for them".

When the final phase kicks in (despair), the business starts looking a little worn around the edges. There is no time or energy to make everything look perfect; there is no one to do the marketing when you are all tied up doing the maintenance;   the living-breathing entity that was your business is a slightly tarnished, paint-peeled, smudged image of its former self.

Getting "Fired"

So what do you do about it? If you are identifying with this, then keep reading. Before we are done we are going to "fire" you – and you will love it!

If you are not already in business, you are very lucky. You get to start a living, breathing entity that may – or may not – hire you, but one that will have its own reason to live to reward you.

So, once you are "fired" (stop working in the business as an employee), then what? The steps are laid out in the pages that follow, but suffice it to say, regardless of what job you think you are doing today, you are going to become a marketer – along with everyone else on your payroll, by the way.

As Dan Kennedy said in his book, *No B.S. Business Success*, "Nobody gets rich dusting shelves, changing light bulbs, keeping books or managing employees. … The place for you to direct your time, energy, creativity, common sense, hard work and resources is marketing." (In Chapter 17 you will learn that *everything* is marketing.)

Getting you out of *The Job* is The Objective.

CHAPTER 4

Are You the Doer, the Overseer or the Entrepreneur?

Every owner of a business has an approach to the business that is derived from his or her core personality. This personality is developed early in life and is essentially "hard wired" into the psyche of the individual.

In the tire business where there may be a generational transition, the patterns of Gen Two often reflect the habits of Gen One.

As I describe the three types of business-owner personalities, you will see people you know and probably yourself – and maybe your parents.

The challenge for most people will be "rewiring" the programming to accomplish The Objective. Very few people are "born entrepreneurs". Every business owner has the ability to be an entrepreneur; it's just harder for some than it is for others. And, many will give up before they get there.

THE THREE FACES

First, there is the **"Doer"**. This is the guy with the *Job*. This is the guy who gets things done. He has to, because the only one on whom he can rely is himself. Getting things done is his source of happiness, fulfillment and meaning. He wants to be the boss, but he certainly does not want to have one. That is why he owns his own business.

Then there is the **"Overseer"**. This is the guy who has outgrown The Job and now has a business to run. Now *that* is The Job! But, it is different than the "Doer" because the "Overseer" organizes the process and cleans up the mess. He perceives himself to be the boss and barely tolerates the idea of having one. That is why he owns his own business.

If "Overseer" does not fit comfortably in your consciousness, you may mentally convert the word to "Manager". The term "Overseer" was intentionally used instead of Manager because of the vague misuse of the term "manager" in common language. Using "Overseer" more graphically defines the behavior characteristics exhibited in this management style.

The third face is the **"Entrepreneur"**. This is the visionary. He needs Overseers (managers) and "Doers" in his operation, but cannot allow himself to be trapped into being either. He creates the systems for the Overseers to execute and the Doers to perform. He is the boss – unless he starts managing or doing. When he does, he stops being the entrepreneur.

Who's at the Top?

In all small businesses there is one person at the top; the final decision-maker. In the description above and the discussion below, it is easy to slip into the idea that we are talking about a hierarchy with three types of people in the same business, the entrepreneur at the top, the Overseers managing operations and the Doers doing the work.

To think this way would be missing the point. The fact is there are very few true entrepreneurs running businesses today. There are far more Overseers in charge – but, remember they also have the title of President. Over two-thirds of businesses are run by Doers who are also called the President. Therein lies the huge challenge.

The Three Faces In Practice

Let's look at how these three faces manifest themselves in real life in more detail:

VISION. The **Entrepreneur** creates a picture of what the business should look like at some point in the future and sets about changing the business to make it match that picture.

The **Overseer** runs the business and repairs damage when it occurs, while steadily moving it forward. His future is in terms of the next payroll, monthly report or quarterly summary.

The **Doer** does not think in future terms. He is committed to keeping things exactly the way they are today. His vision is right in front of him.

OPERATIONAL PROCESSES. The **Entrepreneur** creates them. They are part of his system. They are the gears in his machine.

The **Overseer** organizes them. He does not always see them as part of a whole but, he uses them to get things done.

The **Doer** plays with them. If one thing does not work, he tries another. There is no real consistency and one crisis creates a new operational process until something else happens so he can adjust it or create a new one.

OPPORTUNITIES. The **Entrepreneur** finds them or invents them. They are his main source of entertainment. They are his constant companions.

The **Overseer** sees opportunities differently. They are problems for him. They mess up his comfortable world. They represent more things for him to manage. This can't be good.

The **Doer** greets opportunities with suspicion. They are overwhelming for the does who is far too busy doing what he is doing now. Opportunities are distracting.

CHANGE. It is the **Entrepreneur** who *expects* change. He relishes it because change creates more opportunities. It is the fodder for his imagination. Change is a wonderful thing to the entrepreneur.

The **Overseer** sees change much like he sees opportunities. Change creates havoc in the way "things are done". Change should wait until he is ready to accommodate it. For the **Doer** change simply is not possible. He is far too busy doing what has to be done now to accommodate anything new. He will ignore it.

THINKING. The **Entrepreneur** is always thinking. It is his job. Thinking creates the vision from which all opportunities spring. Thinking is why an entrepreneur gets out of bed in the morning.

The **Overseer** is a little more pragmatic. This thinking thing is OK, but only about the current operation; the things for which he has responsibility. He does not want to think outside of these self-imposed boundaries.

The **Doer** would prefer not to think. Thinking is not work. And, there is always work to do. He knows what to do and how to do it. Why think about anything else?

PROFITS. The **Entrepreneur** creates a machine that produces profits that will attract a future buyer of the business.

The **Overseer** directs a machine that produces profits that make him proud.

The **Doer** works to produce money to live on.

INNOVATION. Innovation is the lifeblood of the **Entrepreneur**. If he does not create it, he finds people with whom to associate who can. It is the raw material for his entire world.

The **Overseer** is OK with innovation as long as it fits. If it makes his current activities easier or better, bring it on. If it changes the course of what he is doing, innovation is a little more problematic.

The **Doer** is not a fan of innovation. *Doing* things is what moves the world forward, not thinking up new things. There is too much to do to be innovating new things.

DISRUPTION. The **Entrepreneur** loves disruption. It is his sport. He makes the messes.

The **Overseer** puts up with disruption. It gives him purpose. He cleans up the messes.

The **Doer** hates disruption. He can only focus on one thing at a time. He avoids the messes as much as possible -- but, often lives in one.

PARTS OF THE WHOLE. The **Entrepreneur** sees his business in the entirety and drills down to the parts.

The **Overseer** sees the parts of the business as the spokes of the wheel with him in the middle.

The **Doer** has all these parts which he mentally collects as the whole, but on which he can, generally, only work on one at a time.

CONTROL. The **Entrepreneur** is seriously into control. He creates systems to establish control in his business world. Control allows him the freedom to think, innovate and disrupt.

The **Overseer** maintains order. If he is in a team with an entrepreneur, his order comes from the entrepreneur's control. On his own, he is not in control beyond what he can manage himself.

The **Doer** does not worry about control. He is doing it all himself anyway. There is nothing to control except himself. His world is limited to that which he is doing. There is always plenty to do.

TENSE. The **Entrepreneur** lives in the Future tense. Everything is an opportunity. Everything is focused on Tomorrow.

The **Overseer** lives in the Past tense. What he does today is determined by what he did in the past -- Yesterday.

The **Doer** mostly lives in the Present tense. Everything he thinks about is right in front of him -- Today.

PSYCHOLOGY. The **Entrepreneur** is the dreamer. Anything is possible.

The **Overseer** is wary. Anything can happen.

The **Doer** is the worrier. Anything can be trouble.

Perhaps you recognize yourself as one of these three "faces". Clearly the majority of business owners today are Doers. A sizable number, perhaps 25 percent, are Overseers. Relatively few, somewhere in the range of five percent are Entrepreneurs.

There is no expectation that a Doer will wake up an Entrepreneur – even if he reads this book three times. There is the absolute probability that the Doer or Overseer will find him or herself dramatically changing the way they do or manage things if they have a clear understanding of what an Entrepreneur is. Picking up a dozen tips and shifting their strategies accordingly will move any business owner much closer to The Objective of freeing him or herself from the daily grind and growing the business to a point where it is less dependent on the owner to make things run.

As you review the descriptions of the Three Faces above you will see a pattern. The Entrepreneur takes an expansive and inclusive view of the business. The Overseer runs the business with not much view of the past or future, all the while keeping the train on the track. The

Doer simply does. And, does. And, does. Anything other than the task at hand is a distraction.

The Entrepreneur integrates the elements of the business into his vision. The Overseer manages the elements for which he is responsible. The Doer sees the elements as his job to get done.

Your business will be in constant chaos without a true vision and plan for growth and profitability. If you do not already have that "entrepreneurial gene", it will be uncomfortable at first to separate yourself "the mechanic" from yourself "the business owner." However, only when you can see your business as an independent entity can you ever hope to be free from the daily responsibility of running it. Only then will the freedom that all business owners seek be possible. It is The Objective.

CHAPTER 5

Is it Really a Risk?

"The real objective of an entrepreneur is to *manage* risk, not *take* risk."

-- Dan Kennedy

Quite often when asked to define an entrepreneur, people will associate the term *risk* with their definition. *Risk Taker, Risk Manager, Willing to take risks.*

In this chapter we will set aside the "Three Faces" definition for a minute and resolve to define every business start-up as an entrepreneurial enterprise regardless of the status of the owner in the *Entrepreneur / Overseer / Doer* trilogy.

The late quintessential entrepreneur, Wilson Harrell (*For Entrepreneurs Only*) made the shocking declaration that entrepreneurs *never* take risks. "The entrepreneur who knowingly takes risks", Harrell stated, "is a fool."

The entrepreneur never takes a risk because he or she, of all the people in the world, is *sure* that the idea will work. Absolute conviction! Can't lose! Sure thing!

Harrell goes on to point out that the entrepreneur's wife may think he is taking a risk. The entrepreneur's banker will see the risks. The entrepreneur's friends, relatives, former fellow co-workers and suppliers will see the risks. But, not the entrepreneur.

If you are Gen Two and want to take the family business into an exciting new direction, you have confidence in your direction. It is Gen One that sees the risk and provides the resistance.

Pam Gatto, President of Gatto' Tires and Auto Service based in Melbourne, Florida describes the wrenching decision to stop being Gatto's Goodyear and establish a local brand. Mike Gatto had been a Goodyear guy from his earliest days in the business, first as an employee and then as a loyal dealer. Pam jokes that a minor cut would produce blue and yellow blood from Mikes wound.

Mike was pretty sure that taking down the massive Goodyear sign and replacing it with Gatto's Tire would cause the earth to stop spinning. Customers would abandon them in droves. And, he would lose friends. You see Mike comes from the generation where loyalty was part of life. People were loyal to the companies for whom they worked and companies were loyal back. As a Gen Two, Pam's view was that the world had changed.

With absolutely no disrespect for Mike's view of the world, shrinking sales made Pam insist that a multi-brand dealership was the way of the future. She eventually won the hard-fought battle and Gatto's Tire has grown every year since.

Pam's vision earned her Entrepreneur of the Year in Florida in 2010.

Such confidence is essential for any business to ever get started. Rarely does anyone start a business to "try it out to see if it works". Because he has analyzed the challenge and built a plan, the entrepreneur does not see himself taking risks.

SELF CONFIDENCE VS. BLIND OPTIMISM

While the entrepreneur tends not to see the risks, there is no assumption that he is a fool either. The danger in blind optimism is that, of course, you could be wrong.

You see it every day. The corner location where "nothing goes" is the new home to an ethnic grocery with a limited population from which to draw. In your head, you say, "I wonder how long … ".

Self confidence, on the other hand, is vital to the prospect of the business getting off the ground. Without the dream and the confidence that the dream can be achieved, no business gets started.

Blind optimism, on the other hand, is misplaced self confidence. It is confidence without foundation. So what is the difference?

OPTIMISM + INFORMATION = CONFIDENCE

Take optimism and add information to create confidence. To have confidence, however, you must have adequate information. That is where research comes in.

RESEARCH

This chapter is devoted to the concept of risk and research. Research minimizes risk; it makes risk manageable; it reduces risk. It reliably shifts optimism to confidence.

Referencing Wilson Harrell again, he coached his small business clients to try the "Well, I'll be Damned Test". The test is amazingly easy and accurate. Take your new idea to 20 potential *buyers* – not family and friends, but people who could prospectively buy the product of your idea – show it to them and see how they react. If they do not say something reasonably close to "Well, I'll be damned!" or "Why didn't I think of that?" you may want to take a pass on your idea and try the next one. To change the world – and move you toward The Objective – your idea must have "Gee Whiz!" power with people in a position to write a check for it.

Dan Kennedy has a set of rules in his *No BS Guide to Business Success*. One of those rules is "Do NOT trust your own judgment".

WHEN TO CONDUCT RESEARCH?

This could be a short section: *Every step along the way.* But, there is more.

Of course, all business plans are based on research. To discover the opportunity, research is required. To describe a path where the business is headed, research is required. To get funding from any knowledgeable source (assume family money is excluded here), research is essential. So, of course, research is vital to getting started.

But, this book, while helpful to prospective owners, is not generally directed at start-ups. There is not even a chapter on "The Business Plan" because that topic is covered extensively in other literature. Chapter 9 suggests some adjustments to your existing business plan, but does not get you started from scratch.

As I was researching this book, I talked to many people in the tire business, several of whom appear on the back of this book. Consensus in the industry is that relatively few people in the tire business have formal, written business plans. If you are in that number, know you are in the majority and do not despair.

While this text may motivate you to start recording your plans, doing so may not be critical. What *is* critical is that you have a good understanding of what is going on outside your store. Knowing trends, opportunities, threats and technology as they may impact your business, is extremely important.

To not do so is to risk being on the sidelines when an opportunity comes along that may change your life.

So, if research applies to start ups, how does it apply to going businesses? *Every step along the way.*

The aware business owner is mostly cognizant of the fact that he or she does not know it all. The aware business owners know that they do not know – the most enlightened position of all. Who could know it all? You say you have met them!? They generally don't stay around too long.

So, assuming you are interested in being around for a while, even growing the business to the point where it does not rely on you for daily survival, research is vital. In fact, the ultimate goal of any true entrepreneur is to establish the business to the point where he is free to do constant research – either to expand what he is doing now or discover what to do next. The entrepreneur is always living in the future. The future is revealed through imagination -- and research.

RESEARCH IS AN ON-GOING PROCESS

There is an endless supply of information flowing at every business person. Sometimes it is only necessary to step into that flow. Reviewing the "Three Faces" you may realize that the Doer has little chance of getting caught up in the flow of information because he or she is far too busy making a living in the business. Without him or her, business would simply stop.

HINT: The enlightened Doer *does* stop and close the business for a few days to do the research. The enlightened Overseer may let loose of the reins for a few days to do the same thing. Unfortunately, it is all too rare. And, thus, the cycle continues for the Doer and the Overseer.

The Entrepreneur seeks sources of information that are not always immediately in his path. He is always looking for new facts, a new relationship, a new source, a new Oracle. Where do they look? Here are a few examples:

THE MORNING NEWSPAPER

The first research of the morning is often in the front yard. The aware entrepreneur is always alert for new developments, trends or events. Those closest to home are the easiest ones to which the aware entrepreneur can react.

The morning paper will have competitors' tire ads; may announce a community event in which the owner can be involved and, thus, gain exposure; it could tell of local state or national legislation that could dramatically impact a tire dealer. Skim it, if you must, but do so daily.

A NATIONAL NEWSPAPER

Newspapers that focus more globally such as the *Wall Street Journal, the International Tribune, Investors' Business Daily*, or *USA Today* offer information about new trends or upcoming events. The aware entrepreneur will use these as regular resources of research.

SUPPLIER SALESPEOPLE

Those who work for your suppliers and call on others who are in your business or related businesses will have knowledge that they may be eager to share. Treating suppliers as teachers rather than *vendors* will pay off generously in terms of information. There is the side benefit of better service and maybe better terms when you demonstrate your respect for their knowledge. While you would never expect an ethical salesperson to share confidential information with you – and you can destroy them as a source if you ask them to – there is lots of information that is not confidential. This is information you would never get as quickly as you would when you have a respectful relationship with those who provide you with supplies and services.

So the next salesperson that shows up in your office should be offered a chair and a cup of coffee. Develop that friendship that goes beyond buyer-seller. Casually, but purposefully, pick his or her brain for ideas, news, gossip and trends. He is not a salesman, he is a news source. Maybe a databank.

SHOP

Go to your competitors' tire stores. Look at how they do business. What good things can you emulate? What bad things can you exploit by contrast? There is nothing un-ethical about shopping.

If you feel you will be recognized, send a staff member with a checklist of things to observe -- and encourage him or her to notice what you haven't listed, too.

NOTE: There is a limit to how far to push this. It gets down to ethics. Do not ever have a competitor spend his resources to provide you with information. Observe, take notes and be polite, if engaged. Stop. That means not taking up a significant amount of a salesman's or esti-mator's time and certainly not taking sample materials that would otherwise go to legitimate customers. Do unto others... .

CALL AROUND

You or someone on your staff can call competitors' busi-nesses and ask questions. You will be amazed at what information you can get just by asking

SHOP OR CALL YOUR OWN BUSINESS

Another source of great insight can come from pretending to be a prospective customer for your own business. Call the business and ask questions typical of a prospective customer. You will get a life-sized view of what your customers are experiencing. If you are concerned about being recognized, have someone else do it while you listen.

ONLINE SEARCH

There are hundreds of search engines available but, for our purposes, we will convert the noun "Google" into a verb. Google yourself. Google your business. Then Google everyone you can think of in your industry. Do not start with any particular information goal, just do the searches. This scavenger hunt can pay off dividends that will surprise you. Clip and save whatever you find that might pay off in the future. The good news is that doing the same searches 30 days from now will reveal new and different results. Change is constant.

Notice, too, who shows up in "Google Places". Do you? (It is absolutely free and absolutely necessary. Do it today, if you have not already.)

NOTE: If you are uncertain about how this works, check in at **www.thetirebusiness.biz** where there are instructions for setting your business up in "Google Places". There is also much information about why this is important and how to manage your image on line, too.

TRADE ASSOCIATIONS

The Tire Industry Association (TIA) is an active and vibrant organization that is an asset to every tire business. Its Executive Vice President, Dr. Roy Littlefield is a significant contributor to this book.

According to Dr. Littlefield, TIA boasts over 5,700 members who own over 15,000 locations. About half of the members, however, own a single location.

Despite the impressive number of members, the surprise is that there are not thousands more given the size of the industry. If you are among those not yet a member of TIA, there are significant money-making (and saving) reasons to do so.

TIA benefits are broad and varied. TIA publishes periodicals with information specifically about the tire industry, for example (a great research source); the organization provides education and training, advocacy with government agencies which impact your business and provides annual conferences to bring members of the industry together.

More than any other single thing you can do, attending industry meetings provides you with the opportunity to meet people in your business that are almost always willing to share ideas and suppliers who have new and different products and services about which you may not be aware. As above, when we discussed supplier salespeople, if you go into a trade exhibit with the idea that every booth contains a teacher rather than a salesperson, your entire experience of the exhibit will change.

Perhaps more than most trade associations, TIA is a significant source of training, not only for owners, but for your staff members. In an industry that is fraught with government meddling and replete with customer satisfaction and genuine safety issues, such training is very much like cash in your bank account – not really income, but a good preventer of unnecessary expenses.

To contact TIA:

Tire Industry Association
1532 Pointer Ridge Place, Suite E
Bowie, MD 20716-1883
www.tireindustry.org

DIRECTORIES
One additional benefit to TIA is that you gain access to membership directories where you can locate people in the tire business you have never met, but who may be willing to talk, share ideas or collaborate in non-competitive markets.

GOVERNMENT PUBLICATIONS
The U.S. Government spends millions of dollars conducting statistical research on every manner of business. While these statistics are broad and general, they can often

reveal trends if you know what you are looking for. Generally, you will be on a research path that defines what you are looking for before you go to secondary data such as that provided by government sources. Still, do not over-look it. You will find printed government statistics in most large city or university libraries. Much government data is online, too.

Although not a Government Agency, the *Encyclopedia of Business* consolidates many government numbers and interesting background information related to the tire business on a free on-line page. The link is long and complicated, but can be accessed using this truncated URL: **www.tiny.cc/tire-data**

NETWORKING
Attending TIA and regional tire association meetings is like free money. Approached correctly, it would be difficult *not* to get your investment back many times. You cannot afford to miss events devoted to your business – ever!

INTERNAL DOCUMENTS
Much can be learned in your own organization. Look for trends in buying patterns and shifts from years earlier. Data that is right under your nose.

Risk is reduced by knowledge. The vast majority of this information is absolutely free. The enlightened entrepreneur knows that he does not know. All too often the small business person already knows it all – or is too busy working in the business to find out.

TRADE PUBLICATIONS

Like most trade associations, TIA publishes a magazine for its members titled, *Today's Tire Industry*. In addition, some of the best information often comes from independent sources. Three of the largest distribution magazines, all of which are free to qualified members of the trade include:

Modern Tire Dealer
Bobit Business Media
3515 Massillon Rd. Suite 350
Uniontown, OH 44685
Subscribe: **www.tiny.cc/subscribe-mtd**

Tire Review
Babcox Publications
3550 Embassy Parkway
Akron, OH 44313
Subscribe: **www.tiny.cc/subscribe-tr**

Tire Business
Crain Communications
1725 Merriman Road, Suite 300
Akron, OH 44313
Subscribe: **www.tiny.cc/subscribe-tb**

GENERAL BUSINESS MAGAZINES

Ideas come from many sources. The publication does not have to relate to the tire business specifically to be of benefit to you. Often the best ideas come from a parallel universe. Something common in one business may have not yet been considered by another. And, since the core of entrepreneurism is growth, that growth can come just as easily from adaptation as it can from innovation. Magazines devoted to small business like *Inc., Entrepreneur* or *Success* will usually be more relevant to the entrepreneurial enterprise than business magazines devoted to the global business picture like *Business Week*, or the *Wall Street Journal*. Just because they have a more global view, however, they should not be ignored.

BOOKS

Well, you are reading this one, so what is there to say? General business books or any non-fiction book that deals with issues that expand your horizon can be fodder for the imagination and should be included in the daily diet of research for your business.

While there do not seem to be too many books written specifically for the business of the tire business, one tire industry veteran has focused significant attention on the small business owner. Tom Gegax, tire industry entrepreneur (a real one!), author, speaker and consultant wrote a book entitled, *The Big Book of Small Business*. It is available for order from Amazon. To simplify getting right to the specific page that describes Tom's book, all you need to do is type: **www.tiny.cc/gegax-book**

THE GOOD NEWS

I have been in the business of writing for small business owners for years. I have witnessed the joys and tragedies experienced by business owners in a wide range of businesses. Economic downturns impact small businesses disproportionately, it seems.

Not so, apparently, in the tire industry. In my extended conversations with Wayne Croswell past president of the Tire Industry Association, I learned what should have been more apparent to me; people buy tires when they can't buy cars. People spend more on service when they need to keep the cars they own up and operating. Of any business that may actually benefit from an economic downturn, the tire business may be one of the few.

That is not to ignore that all smaller businesses are challenged, but later when you read about Krispy Kreme, you might feel better after all.

CHAPTER 6

What Are Your "Anti-Success" Forces?

Thirty years ago, Joe Sugarman (of more recent Blue-Blocker Sunglasses fame) wrote a book titled *Success Forces*. It dealt with certain behavior patterns that a successful business person might undertake to increase the probabilities of success. Many of his ideas were simple, but very effective, such as leaving your desk completely clean each day – which meant you had to have a specific place to put everything away – which also meant you had to provide your team with a place to store their things, too. The result was the mental preparation for an organized start to every day.

The title of his book spawned the title of this chapter, "Anti-Success Forces". There are dozens of people in your environment who are actually pulling against you. Some of them are on your payroll. Some might be in your own family – especially if you are in a multi-generational management situation – whether they intend to or not. Some of them you create in the natural process of growth. You will add more as you implement changes necessary to achieve The Objective. Some are just petty jealousies. Most of them are invisible to the business owner until he or she is trained to look for them. This chapter will serve as your hunting guide.

You have heard it so often you are tired of it, but most people who start businesses fail. And, most people who go to Las Vegas lose. But, planeloads of them arrive every day. And, thousands of businesses open their doors every year. Why do people do this when the odds are so stacked against them?

Frankly, if it were easy, anybody could do it. And, we know everybody cannot. It takes a special person to make a business successful. It takes an entrepreneur to make a business grow beyond the manager who simply wanted a job. Whether or not you qualify as an entrepreneur, thinking like an entrepreneur can make a significant difference in the success of any project.

IT'S A LONELY JOB

Entrepreneurs are lonely. The most successful ones, any-way. They are almost always at cross-purposes with the people in their lives. People from which they must sometimes create separation just to get the job done. Employees, who want more, yet do not come to the table with the full effort. A spouse who creates some sort of an emotional balance scale that suggests you love the business more than you love him or her. Friends who teasingly call you a "workaholic" as they leave the pressures of their job at 5:00 in the afternoon. It does not seem like anyone really understands. This chapter will make you feel better.

ENTREPRENEURIAL INSANITY

Entrepreneurs are generally intelligent people. They know how they are viewed by employees, spouses and friends. That view is not always what they would like it to be. The entrepreneur seems to laugh it off. But, not really. Entrepreneurs are lonely. Lonely because no one really understands the passion they feel for their drive for success. Sometimes the entrepreneur does not understand it either. The insanity comes from trying to please everyone and generally pleasing no one – including the entrepreneur.

The irony of it is that the entrepreneur, at some level, believes what he or she is doing will benefit each of those people in his life – but, they never seem to understand that. The entrepreneur genuinely wants his employees to earn more and gain more autonomy, but they need to buy the vision and contribute to the success with almost blind loyalty.

The entrepreneur genuinely wants his spouse to share the fruits of the labor; to be there when the job is "finished" and the freedom to travel and play finally arrives. But, the spouse must have the patience to wait until that day – if it ever comes.

The entrepreneur genuinely wants to go home at 5:00 like the friends who tease him about his "workaholism". He wants to take time to barbeque on Saturdays and watch football on Sundays. But, those things must wait until the business is "ready".

Success requires emotional independence before the entrepreneur can enjoy financial independence.

Sadly, employees, spouses and friends are not as patient as the entrepreneur. All too often the people closest to the entrepreneur become his greatest *anti-success forces*.

Even more sadly, the committed entrepreneur has to take steps to protect him or herself from them. The committed entrepreneur sometimes needs different employees, new friends and, all too often, he or she will lose a spouse.

Let's look at each of these important influences:

SPOUSES

Don't misunderstand this message. It is not a recommendation to the reader that to succeed he or she must get a divorce. It is a statistical fact, however, that the rate of divorce among entrepreneurs is higher than that of the average population. Money and personal time are great incendiaries for matrimonial discontent. If you are an entrepreneur, you may be able to prepare your life-mate in advance of starting the business. If you are already in the business, he or she already knows, but probably does not understand. Be careful what you promise.

If you are the spouse of the entrepreneur, it may be helpful to understand that he or she does not love you any less because of the business. The business is a different passion.

It does not replace personal passion – unless you decide that it must. That is when the problems start. If you can join the dream, even if you don't join the company (usually a bad idea anyway), your marriage will outlast the formative years of the business into a rich, full life.

The only reason that the odds are against this is there are few couples with the tools to talk it out sufficiently to make it work. Those who do are rewarded multi-fold.

To pull this off, you must have established a clear statement of your goal – Define The Objective. At least you and your spouse will know what you are talking about, will have an idea of what it will "cost" to get there (we are not talking money, here) and will have a reasonable idea of whether or not you are succeeding. Coming back to remembering The Objective when things get rough is one possible way of regrouping more quickly.

FRIENDS

Entrepreneurism is not for the thin-skinned. You will take your share of criticism from even those well-meaning friends who think you are "insane" to do what you are doing. More often than not, these friends are "stuck" in their own jobs and are secretly jealous of your "freedom". (No, they don't understand.) Also, you will note, they are also the same ones who are first to ask for a deal on tires!

Good natured ribbing may be OK in the short term, but when it starts to wear you down; when you begin to make decisions based on what others will think or say, then it is time to get some new friends. Time spent around negative, fearful, skeptical, doubtful people will sap your strength. It will damage your resolve to achieve The Objective, Remember: Freedom! (The freedom your friends already *think* you have!)

If you are thin-skinned and the opinions of the well-meaning (or maybe not so well-meaning) friends begin to impact your decision making, it is time to get a "real job" and stop pretending to be an entrepreneur. You will be miserable otherwise.

But, there will be those around you who are loyal to your dreams and support you when you need it. These people are your gifts from the Universe. You must keep them close so they can nurture you – and you, them.

The move away from the negative people does not have to be as dramatic as slamming a door. You just choose to spend the time you have with different people – or with no one who does not "get it". Do this out of respect for your own resolve to achieve The Objective. Believe it or not, you don't even need to seek out new friends. They will find you. They will find you in some sort of natural process. When you make the **Declarative Statement** it happens faster. More on that at the end of this chapter.

EMPLOYEES

These can be the easiest and the hardest of your *anti-success forces* with which to deal.   They are the easiest because you are buying their time for a fee and can simply stop buying it. (Few business people think about employees as fee-for-service, but it is far healthier for the business when you do.) When they are not a profitable investment, you simply stop buying their services.

It is harder when these same employees are the ones who were with you when you put the first dollar into the cash drawer. Your pioneers. Often, your friends. But, make no mistake about it, they are *not* your partners. If the place goes down, they lose a job; you lose your life savings.

There have been many articles written about employees who manage the boss through subtle and insidious black-mail. The bookkeeper that knows more about the process than the owner; the shop manager who knows the sources better than the owner; the service writer who has more contact with and personal rapport with key customers than the owner; the purchasing manager who has the special relationships with the distributors that the owner knows nothing about.

These specialists are valuable to any company. They are often complimented and bragged about by the owner to visitors and bankers.

"Joe is the best service manager in the state. We could not get along without him." And, Joe believes you!

All is well, until one day Joe is gone. Two-week notice, if that. New job. New opportunity. Giant X Tire Company was willing to pay to get the 'best service manager in the state'. And, he takes a stack of customers with him. It's nothing personal, of course, just a better opportunity.

Except it *is* personal!! You trained and mentored them. You complimented and loved them. You took care of them when they had special needs.

And, they are gone. Just like that!

You shake your head. While your objective was to achieve more personal freedom by hiring and nurturing these employees, it turns out *they had more freedom than you do!*

There is nothing wrong with solid, loyal employees. But, there is a way to have them and grow with them, but never be held hostage by them. It gets down to *Systems*. Systems that you get to create and control. Systems that are independent of any individual.

How do you think a company like McDonald's can experience turnover of over 200 percent a year and not miss a beat? It is because there is a *way* every little thing is done – independent of who is doing it.

Michael Gerber stated it succinctly in the *E-Myth*, when he suggested the world is not generally populated with extraordinary people. Most employees are ordinary people. Successful businesses employ ordinary people using *extra-ordinary systems*.

More About Employees

Larry Morgan may be one of the best entrepreneurs the tire industry has ever seen. In fact, since selling his tire interests that ultimately included over 600 stores, Larry has proven himself to be an amazing entrepreneur in a range of businesses including new car sales for Toyota. In 2010, Larry was named Florida Dealer of the Year by TIME magazine, Goodyear and NADA.

Morgan acknowledges the harsh realities of labor in the tire business. He said that as his empire grew larger his ultimate role was that of "Big Glorified Human Resources Manager". In the service business, it all gets down to the people.

In describing his philosophy of labor at the store level, Morgan stated emphatically that, "incentive compensation is mandatory in the tire business. ... But, to be successful, the system must be extremely simple to understand and implement."

Getting employees to think like owners is a losing game. They are not owners. If they could be, you might do well not to hire them anyway. They would not stay and you would pay to train them to quit and ultimately run their own business.

Getting employees to think in their own self-interest is not nearly as challenging. That is central to Larry Morgan's advice about incentive compensation. Here is where the owner and employee become aligned. The more profitably and efficiently an employee works, the more money he or she makes. If the system is unambiguous and there is no sense of "negotiation" at the end of a pay period, everything runs along smoothly.

Properly structured, a compensation plan for service personnel can be a fixed percentage of department income. Predictable for the owner; satisfactory for the employee.

ALTERNATIVE COMPENSATION MODELS

Pam Gatto, whom you met earlier heads up a seven-unit group of retail tire stores in Florida. She describes her incentive program as one in which the service personnel receive a negotiated hourly wage with an incentive of 10 percent "commission" on all work performed. This, Gatto reasons, keeps the work moving more efficiently when the employees eagerly accomplish one task to earn commissions on the next one.

An alternative described by Wayne Croswell, president of WECnology and past president of the Tire Industry Association, that some of his clients use, is one in which the employee is paid a percentage of the "standard book rate or flat rate" regardless of how long a job takes.

The theory is that the employee will be ultimately in charge of his hourly rate by how efficiently he works. On jobs that run smoothly, everybody wins. On challenging jobs, everybody loses. But, everybody along the line, customer, owner and employee, knows exactly what their respective costs will be all along the way.

WORK OR PLAY?

The thing that so few people understand about entrepreneurs is that they never see themselves as workaholics. Their friends do not see themselves as jealous and resentful, either. Those friends see their own employment as a job. The entrepreneur sees work as play. It is the sport. And, as in any sport, a score is kept. For Doers and Overseers the score is usually dollars. For entrepreneurs the score is more often kept by measuring the number of hours *not* running the business, but working on growing it, and eventually letting it run itself. The dollars just seem to happen.

THE DECLARATIVE STATEMENT

The entrepreneur's Dream is his constant companion. Earl Nightingale said, "We become what we think about most." To create the Dream and hang on to it in the face of so many anti-success forces can be an act of courage. Some give it up. Let it die. It is just too hard.

73

While the Dream is often quite private, there is another way to look at it – as a tool. A tool that can quiet or at least quell the impact of most of the anti-success forces in your universe. To do this, you make a Declarative Statement.

Tell the world what you plan to do. Share the dream.

Sure you will still have nay-sayers and detractors. Actually, being open about your vision lets you spot them more easily. At least they will know what they are nay-saying about. All too often the entrepreneur plays it so close to the vest, the detractors in their world don't really even know what they are detracting. They have to come to some oblique assessment like, "you work too many hours", but have no idea what you are working on.

Once you make your Declarative Statement, you will be subject to scoffing by those who see you as you are, not as you will be. Ignore them. Do not allow them to cast you into self-doubt. After all, it is not their Dream, it is yours!

You will attract a larger number of supporters including most – but, not all – of your employees when you have made a Declarative Statement. People who have something to contribute will be more willing to share – when they know where you are headed.

The process is very much like marketing research. Once you have stated clearly what you wish to accomplish, you will get feedback in ways you did not ever expect. Listen.

But, know that anti-success forces will be among the feedback you get. Filter what you take to heart carefully. Do not get dragged down by doubt when those who know less about your project than you do take shots at it.

But, then, do not close your ears to contrary ideas either. Not all of those who disagree with you will do so with real or imagined malice.

One of the benefits of the Declarative Statement is that you will attract mentors who can truly help you, too. Once you "put it out there", your Declarative Statement will attract all sorts of attention. You will grow as a result. Listen.

NOTE: One of the by-products of this book is to identify the subset of tire business owners who "get it" and want to start a path toward growth – and freedom. Toward that end, a group called "**Tire Entrepreneurs of North America**" (TENA) has been formed.

If you would like to know more, go to **www.thetirebusiness.biz** and register for free. You will find resources that will help you. In addition, non-competitive groups will be formed for idea exchange and sharing. You are encouraged to visit the TENA site today.

CHAPTER 7

Entrepreneurial Terror; Thought you were the only one?

In the last chapter we talked about the loneliness of being an entrepreneur. The business owner is the only one who is truly on the line when it gets right down to it. And, this can be frightening.

Rarely does the guy who mounts the tires worry about whether his paycheck will be honored. The business owner is far more likely to worry about making that true.

Rarely does the mechanic worry about whether there is enough stock on the shelf. The business owner is far more likely to worry about making sure the supplier is paid on time to ensure shipment.

Rarely does the service writer concern himself with taxes being due or inspectors halting operations. The business owner is the only one who must deal with these issues.

It is the business owner who makes commitments to investors and bankers. Only the *one in charge* will get the phone call when things go awry.

It all adds up to some potentially terrifying events. But, that is part of the job. It is why achieving The Objective is so rewarding. It means you have developed a team to take the brunt of the problems – and they are trained to handle them exactly as you would if you were there.

Until you get to this point, however, there are going to be a few sleepless nights along the way. Sleepless nights springing from anger, resentment, grief, frustration, disappointment, depression, letdown and, of course, fear. You cannot be in the game without experiencing some or all of these emotions at one point or another. How much time you let them take up from your focus distinguishes the far-sighted entrepreneur from the short-sighted small business owner.

The challenge is exacerbated by the fact that action (or inaction) does not show up in results for days, weeks or months in the future. All too often there is no "quick fix". Sometimes there is a delayed surprise. Imagine the amazement of the pre-historic man when women produced babies! The nine-month distance between the action and the reaction was a total disconnect. Sometimes such disconnects occur with modern business owners, too.

PERSPECTIVE

Earlier you were introduced to Wilson Harrell. Wilson has touched your life even if you did not ever see his name before you picked up this book. If you have ever read *Inc.* magazine, Wilson was its publisher at one time. If you have ever cleaned up with Formula 409, Wilson took a bankrupt provider of a cleaning solution and built it into a multi-million dollar enterprise before selling it to Clorox. You may not have ever tried "Tosta-Pizza" because it flopped – Wilson created that, too.

"Entrepreneurial Terror" is a term borrowed from Wilson Harrell; in fact, it is the title of the first chapter in his book *For Entrepreneurs Only* (Career Press, 1995). In that chapter Wilson writes, "Terror is something that entrepreneurs don't expect, can't escape and have no way of preparing for. … Few people even talk about it. The truth is that those of us who have experienced entrepreneurial terror seldom admit to it. As a result, it remains a deep, dark secret. The terror is so secret, in fact, that each of us thinks he or she is the only one who's ever felt it."

In his many speeches, Wilson used a personal story to put business terror into perspective. His story is being retold here for that same purpose and to honor a man who meant so much to so many of us with his forthright, powerful statements of wisdom; lessons that he personally exper-ienced before delivering them in his presentations.

Paraphrased here, Wilson tells of being shot down behind enemy lines in France during World War II. The French Underground prevented his capture in a unique way that makes the perception of terror all the more poignant. They carried his badly burned body into a corn field, dug a trench and placed Wilson in the trench. They stuck a hose in his mouth and buried him.

He tells of the darkness. He tells of the fear of Germans sticking bayonets down into the earth searching for him or shooting into the earth randomly. He tells of worrying someone would accidentally kick the hose – or turn on the faucet!

When it was safe, the French Samaritans would dig him up and feed him. And, bury him again. For eleven days he "lived" like that.

And, lived he did, to the benefit of so many. We lost Wilson in 2004, but not before he taught us a little perspective about terror.

SOURCES OF TERROR
Feeling That the Whole Thing is Not Real. Leaving the comfort of an employed position can be terrifying, in and of itself. Starting a business from the ground up puts the owner in a starting-from-scratch position with little stability or security. No history to go on and only a business plan for guidance (making the assumption there is one).

To begin with, working for yourself can be disorienting. There is no "boss" to tell you what to do. The days come and go and, without a framework for measuring progress. It can seem like you are adrift.

Besides, by not having a boss, you have no support structure, benefits – or paycheck. Scary stuff.

Some of this anxiety can be alleviated by having written goals on a daily, weekly and monthly basis. Some framework against which you can measure progress. By achieving even elementary goals, the sense of "realness" sets in and soon confidence grows.

Failing your family. So many people in the tire business are second generation that the impact of family adds to the pressure. Taking over a business that everyone thought was successful (regardless of the reality) is a heavy responsibility with plenty of "second-guessers" close at hand. This can be disconcerting, if not terrifying.

The Overall Economy. Being on your own in recent years has been terrifying enough. Borrowing is unpredictable. Customers can disappear at the blink of an eye. Car count you depended on to make payroll or rent is subject to market whims over which you have little or no control. It *is* frightening.

Some business owners, however, see it as an opportunity. When publicly-held companies and larger competitors retrench to meet the expectations of shareholders and lenders, sometimes opportunities open for the smaller, more agile company. This is the company that can make a decision at 4:00 on Monday and be taking action at 9:00 Tuesday morning.

This is why keeping a close eye on the daily paper for "Big Box" tire ads and staying in touch with local business leaders can be an astute strategy. Knowing your competitive and community environments can dramatically improve your strategy and planning.

Loss of Freedom. Ironically, most people start their own businesses to *achieve* freedom. In fact, freedom is The Objective, when it is all said and done. Fear is introduced when the new business owner looks at the distance to be traveled between starting and achieving The Objective. There is lots of work to be done. Not having any time for yourself or your family can be challenging. It can be emotionally divisive. The business needs attention and your family needs attention. Which entity wins? Therein lies the emotional struggle. The fear of that struggle can be debilitating.

Developing a business that can involve your family can have good and bad results. Plus, it allows the family to be more engaged in the process. On the other hand, communication between family members tends to be "less formal" and challenging for non-family members to experience. However, it can be difficult, if not impossible, to fire a family member when necessary.

Being actively involved with others who own businesses can be helpful. Even if you cannot discuss your particular business issues, the camaraderie of having others who are traveling your business-ownership path at the same time can provide support and perspective. There are any number of local business groups you can join. Do so. Sometimes these can produce strategic relationships, too.

Additionally, being in a business that you truly enjoy can ameliorate some of the anxiety. If you love the business, the trade-offs and sacrifices are more easily accommodated when others are walking in your same shoes.

Keeping Your Head Above Water. Cash flow. Start-up money can run thin. Operations, regardless of sales, must be maintained. Growth requires capital. Not knowing where that is coming from creates fear.

The old expression, "Nothing happens until somebody sells something" is dramatically true. You may not consider yourself a salesperson. You hire service writers and sales people to work for you. But, no one can sell with the same vision and passion as the founder. In your case, it is less selling than it is story-telling. You will always be the best salesperson for your company – even when it is not your "real" job.

Cash flow fear is resolved by sales. You are absolutely the shortest distance between the problem and the solution. Never stop selling. Don't stop selling even when you have a whole staff of salespeople. Selling in this context does not necessarily mean cold calling or even taking orders. It means being *out there*. It means telling *the story*. It means

83

not being in the service bays or the office. It means being a visible part of your community, too.

Pay close attention to the story about the baker in the next chapter. He only had to make one "sale" to change his life.

Failing. The humiliation of it! Your friends. Your family. Your former co-workers who watched you tell the boss to take that job and shove it! Failing in your own business is terrifying. Not as much from the loss of cash as your very public failure to achieve the goal.

Yet, 90 percent of new businesses do fail. With odds like that, perhaps there is another reason for terror. Interestingly, however, that number is much smaller (like 20 percent rather than 90 percent) for franchises – businesses built on the concept of *systems*.

Larry Morgan, introduced earlier, suggests that sometimes tire business owners' skills are so far on the technical side that the business simply outgrows their ability to manage it. After the stresses of managing employees and trying to meet the expectations of not-always-reasonable customers, when it gets down to doing all of the rest of the things that go into owning a business, there is just not enough energy or mental capacity to handle it all.

This limitation may be self-imposed, however. So often the fear comes from the "what-if's" in your head. Most of the "what-ifs" do not occur, but they sit out there like the boogey man in the dark.

Viewed another way, however, failure is actually almost a requirement for a truly successful entrepreneur. Some of the greatest names in business history have gone bankrupt (Henry Ford, J.C. Penney, Conrad Hilton, H.J. Heinz, Frank Lloyd Wright, Walt Disney, P.T. Barnum, David Buick (cars), James Folger (coffee), Sam Walton, William Fox (movies).

A study from Tulane University's School of Business suggests that the average entrepreneur fails approximately four times before achieving significant success. It may not be the obvious choice for a path to success, but failure at one thing is hardly the end of the road.

Knowing that reduces terror. Reducing terror makes it easier to succeed.

CREATING YOUR OWN BUFFER

Because entrepreneurs typically work in a sort of isolation, they do not get sufficient perspective. Self-defeating thinking can creep in when there is no one to help sweep it out. Compounded, it can make the business owner increasingly negative and doubtful. Terrified.

Keeping tabs on your successes is a good way to keep perspective. Small successes as well as large ones. The business owner does not always have someone there to provide the "atta-boys" that he got when working at someone else's company. It is one more thing on the list of things the true entrepreneur must learn to do; self-back-patting. No one else is likely to do it for you.

One other key thing to remember about the fear of failure is the difference between *business* failure and *personal* failure. Keeping the two separate is vital for the ability of the entrepreneur to get on to the next project. If it were easy, anybody could to it. Feeling guilt over a business failure is a wasted emotion. If your intentions were honorable throughout, prepare to move on. The successful entrepreneurs have done so – an average of four times each.

THE BURDEN

Perhaps as much as anything, entrepreneurial terror comes from the knowledge that ultimately there is *only you*. There is no one else who has ultimate responsibility for the end result. Larger companies enjoy layers of direct reports so there is always someone to blame. Or, decisions get made by committees where there is no person to blame. Sometimes they hire someone to blame if things go wrong; people who can't get fired. They call them "consultants".

In any business there are lots of excuses. And, you don't get to use them. You generally don't get to tell anyone about the sick baby, frozen lock, power outage, late delivery of products, and the supplier who suddenly shuts down or when UPS goes on strike. You *own* all of the excuses.

86

Before you get all glum about your sorry lot in the equation, understand that part of the Entrepreneurial Insanity process is to anticipate these situations and structure a plan or set of plans that mean that sick babies and power outages are not unfortunate surprises – they are *expected!* It is one more step toward The Objective – making your presence in the business insignificant to its daily operation. It is the cure for the Insanity.

That cure involves the development of a collection of systems to resolve every anticipated problem before it occurs (sick baby, frozen lock, power outage, supplier shut down, UPS strike, delayed payments, OSHA investigations).

There are very few "new" disasters. And, all disasters boil down to the lack of personnel, utilities, funds or facilities. You can start inoculating yourself from terror by having a plan for all the disasters you can think up.

NEVER SHARE TERROR

Before this chapter closes, there is one more important thing to remember: never share terror! Do not try to share it with a friend. If he or she is not an entrepreneur, it is like describing a roller coaster ride to someone who has never been on a roller coaster. They have no real ability to empathize with you. And, it sounds like you are trying to offload your fears on to someone else. Good friends will tend to internalize your angst. Not fair. Strangers don't – and shouldn't – care.

Even more important: it is not wise to share your terror with your loved ones. If they are not working in the business with you, your terror can only make them despondent or even sick. After all, you convinced them that this idea simply could not fail. If it does, they will learn soon enough. And, chances are very good that the situation that created your terror will get resolved before they find out. If it does and you have shared it, the only thing they will remember is the "close call". It is better to keep your secret and see if your fears are justified.

Until then, understand that the terror you feel is just one part of the price for ultimate success.

Every entrepreneur experiences terror. Very few ever talk about it.

CHAPTER 8

Why Are You Keeping
All That Stuff, Anyway?

It is common with creative people -- and entrepreneurs are almost always in that group -- to hang on to excess "junk" because they "just might need it someday" or "it is too valuable to get rid of". I am one of those "creative junk collectors", much to the chagrin of my wife (who is the spouse of an entrepreneur, you know). But, I am getting "the cure".

After a few years of thinking this, but not acting on it, the rational person will face the reality that it really is "junk", no matter how valuable it might theoretically be. If you don't have time to convert it into something useful, it *is* junk.

To some extent tire dealers are fortunate when it comes to the subject of junk. So many components require recycling, most junk goes away systematically.

This still leaves the opportunity to hold onto dead inventory, old unused tools, unfiled paperwork – and all of those yet-to-be-recycled items. To provide the opportunity to make a place look cluttered.

This is another bit of *entrepreneurial insanity*. But, it can, and should, be cured. It is not hard and feels particularly good when the junk is gone. Additionally, your place of business will take on a more streamlined and efficient look. This is always attractive to visitors which can either be clients, prospective clients or potential buyers of your enterprise. You never know when they will appear!

Jody DeVere (AskPatty.com) makes the case that women are particularly attuned to the working/selling environment being comfortable (clean and neat). Given the percentage of women who are tire purchasers, paying attention to this attribute alone, may mean significant contributions to your revenues.

New opportunities and clients come into your life only when there is room for them. While the logistics of this are not obvious, the psychological implications are. The actual clutter (or even neatly stacked and boxed junk), is probably taking up more than physical space. Consider how it makes you feel emotionally perhaps, overwhelmed, frustrated, disorganized, and maybe even lethargic.

What is often the case is that your visual space is so full of junk that you either don't see new opportunities, or you are too crowded to be able to take advantage of them when they appear.

The process takes three steps:

1. **Decide.** Cast off those tendencies to hoard and be clear that you want to clear.

2. **Prepare.** Set up a triage system. Often the process is much easier if the individual involved knows that there is the opportunity to have the excess material go to a worthy cause. So, step two includes that opportunity. It also includes a *failsafe* component if you just cannot decide what to do and want to defer.

   Establish four areas (or boxes, or rooms or whatever). Label each with "Trash", "Donations", "Sell" and "Defer". NOTE: Set some sort of limit (say 10 percent) on the "Defer" area or you will be just moving junk from one pile to another. Also, commit to coming back to the "Defer" box in six months. If you have not used anything from it, it gets moved into the donation or trash pile.

3. **Just do it!** Establish the rules and get your team to-gether for this project. Tackle the smaller areas first to get momentum. Then move to larger projects. You may have to make the process a multi-day project. But, remember your commitment to the clearing and focus on coming back to finish.

As you go through this process remember the objective. You are setting up your business to have a value. A value is established when you know that someone else would pay you money for the opportunity you have created. Look at your business through the eyes of an outsider. If you see junk, you have devalued your business.

Even if you have no intention of selling, if you see junk you will be slowed in the fulfillment of your intentions.

Got junk? Answer no!

CHAPTER 9

What Were You Thinking?

Unless you invested in your business out of personal savings or from trusting friends or family members, or, unless you are part of the Gen Two group, there is a pretty good chance you wrote a business plan. Bankers want to see them even if they don't believe them – and even if you have collateral to back up the loan. Sophisticated invest-ors won't even talk to you without one. And, it is possible that, even if you did not need to raise capital to start your business, you were enlightened enough to prepare one just for yourself.

Even if you have never written a formal business plan, the questions often answered in a business plan that appear in this chapter will give you important things to think about.

And, even if you prepared a business plan at one time, odds are that it has not been updated since you wrote it. This is not always so with new business owners, but certainly it is in the vast majority of cases.

If that is your situation, this chapter should make you a little uncomfortable – at least to start. Uncomfortable because you will remember all of the things you said you would do that you have not quite gotten around to. The numbers you boldly forecasted make you wonder what you could have been thinking at the time. Don't sweat it. You have lots of company. And, there is good news.

Your business plan represented your best hopes at a point in time. You now have something real against which to compare it. Undertaking the rewriting of a business plan is not nearly as daunting as starting one from scratch. And, if you have never written one at all, it is actually pretty easy once you are in the business. There is a lot less guessing when you have experience. And, your numbers will be a lot more realistic!

But, you may ask, why would I want to write a business plan, or even update an old one? The answer goes less to planning than to thinking. Notice the chapter title is What Were You *Thinking*?" not, "What Were You *Planning*?". Using the business plan as a framework simply focuses that thinking more easily. Besides, business plans have had a pretty standard format for years. Ever wonder why?

A NEW LOOK AT AN OLD PLAN

In this chapter we are going to look at a few of the common components of typical business plans and restructure them into points of focus on current challenges you may be facing. By reworking the key elements of a business in your head, you will come away with a clearer awareness of exactly what you need to do to achieve The Objective – less time actually running the business and more time focusing on growing it and having a life of your own.

Typical Business Plan Question #1:
Describe your business and the products or services you plan to offer.

Did you start out selling tires and under-car services? Have you expanded into under-the-hood services, car washing, detailing or ice cream sales? How does the answer to question #1 differ from the day you started? What have you learned in the interim that might have caused a shift, if any? How involved did you plan to be in the day-to-day operation of the store or stores?

With some experience under your belt, can you answer the question of whether you are selling tires or are you in the *business* of selling tires? That question gets right down to the difference between the thinking of a *Doer* or *Overseer* versus an *Entrepreneur*.

As you rewrite this section of the business plan, try to focus on your role as the owner of a *business* that produces or sells your products or services rather than someone who actually does it or actively manages the process. It may not be possible for you to extricate yourself from the process right away, but remember this is a business plan not a contract. Plan what you want to do with your business – and your life – in this exercise.

Doers do. Overseers manage. Entrepreneurs plan.

Typical Business Plan Question #2:

Who are the players in your company and what roles do they fill?

In Chapter 17, we are going to talk about the organization chart and how many of the boxes have your name in them. The exercise leads to planning how to replace your name in all but the top box. For now, simply list the people on your payroll and the jobs they do. Make note of what percentage of their efforts require input from you.

If you have to tell them to do everything that you want done, you might feel important (indispensible) in your role as the head honcho, but, it is a quick ticket to entrepreneurial insanity! You will be totally trapped in your important role and will have absolutely no freedom to do your own work (except after hours when everyone has gone home and you can get some quiet) or take a day off, or take a vacation, or some days, even be able to think!

As you rewrite this section of your plan think hard about those who require the most and the least hand-holding. If you can remember, make a list of the last five questions each of them asked you. Then, for each question, ask yourself if you had a "Policy" (system) to which the employee could have referred before the question was asked, would you have had to be involved at all?

Next, try to "price" each decision you made for the employee. How much would it have cost to allow the employee make his or her own decision – *and be totally wrong*? Rarely are decisions totally wrong, but to prevent even a small percentage, most business owners will not allow that chance. And, it consumes them.

What policies could you put in writing that would eliminate a high percentage of your involvement with the kinds of questions you deal with daily?

It may not seem like much when you are running a single store, but what would happen if you opened a second one, or a dozen, or hundreds? Who would the employees go to for answers? This is the key to a growth mentality. It is the difference between owning a business and owning an asset.

Doers do. Overseers manage. Entrepreneurs guide.

Typical Business Plan Question #3:
Describe your industry, its current and future prospects and how your company will take advantage of these facts. Describe your products or services along with the features and benefits they provide the customer.

Is the industry the same as it was when you started? What changes have occurred? Have your products or services changed since you started?

In the last decade things have changed more than at any time in history. There is no reason to think that the next decade will level off and let you catch your breath. Perhaps your business has changed dramatically since you started. Maybe you had a full tire shop and now sell only commercial tires to a few companies. Maybe you were a commercial tire dealer and now have a full scale automotive service company with several locations.

More likely you are pretty much what you were when you started. Most business owners tend to stick with what they know, and that with which they feel safe. But, it is a double-edged sword.

Jody Devere (AskPatty.com) makes the point that a significant trend in the tire industry is an awareness of tire efficiency. While this can be viewed as a cost-saving argument to customers, it is being marketed in the "Green" movement, as well. Low-rolling-resistance tires improve gas mileage for the car, obviously reducing the cost of fuel and ultimately tires. Saving in these areas reduces the environmental impact of burning fuel which takes an advantage and reframes it for a different audience, all the while taking safety into consideration. It is unlikely that this conversation would have taken place ten years ago.

Without change there is stability – but, only if nothing else around you changes! With change, there is insecurity because everything around you *is* changing. Both of those statements assume you are a victim of the marketplace; that you have no control over events and must live a defensive life. *Doers* and *Overseers* tend to operate in a defensive manner. *Entrepreneurs* take an offensive posture.

The entrepreneur creates a business that allows him to stick his head out of the business long enough to assess the direction of the wind, locate opportunities and steer the ship in the most opportune direction.

Instead of tires, imagine for a moment you were in the bakery business. It would be very easy to continually bake cookies, cupcakes, bread and dozens of other varieties of baked goods that customers eagerly gobble up on a daily basis. The business would have a pretty steady schedule of holidays and birthdays that are reasonably easy to predict. The owners need not worry too much as long as everything remains the same.

Krispy Kreme Donuts launched their massive expansion about two years before a flood of health-related reports came out that made the public much more aware of the impact of sugar and fried dough on their bodies. The sales curves that drove their enthusiasm suddenly started to flatten and then plummet. Planning a continuing flow of new customers clamoring for this unique North Carolina product turned out to be faulty. And, there was no back-up plan, apparently. The stock (NYSE/KKD) that soared to $50 settled to around $3 by fourth quarter 2007 and has stayed in the low single digits ever since. Times changed for Krispy Kreme even though their systems remained fairly consistent.

On the other hand, as the owner of the bakery who spent less time baking, but left behind employees who knew the "recipe" for exactly how the bakery should run every moment of every day, you had the time to attend Chamber of Commerce meetings. There you meet the owner of the new convention hotel in town.

At the next Chamber meeting you just happened to bring fresh French bread for the people on the committee on which you serve – including that hotel owner. The compliments lead to a conversation about supplying the hotel with fresh bread on a daily basis. And, because the newest, biggest hotel in town is a customer, it makes it easier for you to get the attention of dozens of other restaurateurs and hotels, too.

All of a sudden, as the owner of a small retail bakery you are in a position to stop worrying about dozens of items to prepare every day, dealing with waste for unsold product, many of the cyclical highs and lows throughout the year and just have the wholesale customers call in orders daily for a more limited range of products. In the process, you put systems into place that make day-to-day operations run smoothly – regardless of whether you are there or not.

Every aspect of his business becomes more streamlined and predictable – and larger. Growth that seemed impossible for your small retail bakery, simply involved a new truck and expansion to a nearby town with more hotels and restaurants. All you have to do is put the exact same systems into place.

So, as you interpolate donuts into tires, think how the same out of the office mentality can be applied to your business. What strategic relationships are hiding in plain sight?

Allow your imagination to wander to the possibilities, not the limitations.

Doers play defense. Overseers play defense.
Entrepreneurs play offense.

Typical Business Plan Question #4:

What is your growth strategy? How large is your market? What strategies can you employ to exploit the market as it is today vs. what it was when you opened?

Analyzing a market and establishing a strategy is often one of the more difficult tasks for a start-up company. If the business plan is to be presented to others, it is critical to make it plausible. Over-exuberance can lead to doubt among those less engaged with your new ideas than you are. On the other hand, assuming you have been in business for a while, marketing strategy should be a good deal easier. You do not have to guess as much about the market size, trends and the status of competition.

Your review of this topic invites you to look at the subject with a different set of eyes than you did when you first wrote your plan. Back then, it is likely that your vision was narrow and focused. There is nothing wrong with that in a start-up. Few people are capable of broad vision at that phase. It is likely that Sam Walton never dreamed of the scope of his eventual empire when he opened his first general merchandise store in Arkansas. Somewhere along the line, however, he discovered that his style of management could be duplicated. That was the turning point. He evolved from Overseer to Entrepreneur.

Whether you can develop an enterprise the size of Wal-Mart or not, the pattern is the same. Like Sam was a few billion dollars ago, you have been in the business a while and it is time to do something different that will help you achieve The Objective. As you look at your growth strategy, what are the possibilities?

Can you *duplicate* what you are doing in other locations? This is the most typical expansion model, but it may or may not be the most profitable path for you. If you do this, you will need to have the systems down pat.

Can you *expand* what you are doing and develop a whole new set of customers? For example, having a business where customers leave their cars and frequently do not sit and wait for them could open the opportunity to add a line of services made possible with a longer leave-time for the car. This might include washing, waxing or detailing, for example.

Or, if your location is close enough to the airport, offer a series of "while you are gone" services that include keeping the car safe while the owner is away. Allowing the cost of your services to offset the cost of paid parking, might generate more sales – and goodwill.

With expanded profit centers, the need for written systems is increasingly necessary. Growth without systems can be very expensive.

Do you want to *narrow* what you are doing and focus only on the most profitable segment of your business? In the example of our baker, he gave up cookies and cupcakes to expotentially expand his bread business. In this case, the highest and best use of his time was finding additional wholesale accounts, or putting himself in situations where strategic growth opportunities reveal themselves. Specific systems are required to free him to do this so that he is confident that the bread he sells is baked and delivered *exactly* as promised.

Doers and Overseers maintain.
Entrepreneurs grow.

Digging out that old business plan and looking at it with new eyes may clarify a bit of the insanity with which you are living in keeping the business going today. Reviewed within the content of the entrepreneurial mindset, thinking strategically, you are likely to see your business as potentially much larger than you ever have before.

If you do not have an old business plan to dig out and you think it might be a good time to put one together, here are a couple of resources you might find helpful:

How to Write a Business Plan... Made Easy is a $29.70 downloadable book that goes into great detail about all of the elements you should consider and includes sample plans, financial plan worksheets and a quick-start guide. To read about it and access the order form, go to, **www.tiny.cc/business-plan**

If you are not all that keen on writing your plan from scratch, there is a company that publishes pre-written plans that you can take and customize to your situation.

Business Planning 4 You provides a tire-store-specific product that will get you started for $69.95. They offer several bonuses of general, small business background material in the deal. (You will probably want to skip the "free web hosting" offer. Such offers often come with barbed hooks.)

Go to, **www.tiny.cc/tire-business-plan** and take a look. They offer a full business plan which is sent as a word document attachment to your email address within 12 hours of the order being successfully placed. (To preserve copyright protection, each document they prepare is unique in some way which is why it takes a few hours to get it to you.)

You will receive a completed, tire-industry-specific, business plan of approximately 25 pages. You will need to (or want to) revise it to match your own situation.

In addition, they will send a free, relevant, second business plan as well as offer you with free website hosting for a year. The package also includes a "Business Support Package" that supports the elements of a business plan, including Profit & Loss, Startup costs, Balance sheets, Spreadsheets and Cash flow statements that are ready for you to complete, plus 60 other business documents as well.

CHAPTER 10

What Would it Look Like if You Were "Finished"?

In the previous chapter there are several references to the importance of systems to create the freedom needed by the business owner to have time to grow the business. In this chapter we are going to delve deeply into an understanding of what it looks like when you achieve The Objective.

THE MENTAL IMAGE OF SUCCESS

To help you better understand the rationale behind having systems at all and why they are the absolute key to your achieving The Objective, let's do a little "out of body" experience.

Suppose you are outside of your business looking in. You have successfully put your business together and you are considering selling it and doing something else. You are describing it to a stranger – someone who could be a prospective buyer of your business. Properly prepared, you have the freedom to say, "Let me show you how it works!" not "Let me show you what we sell" or "Let me show you what we do". You get to show something very meaningful to a prospective buyer – your *system* for making money.

You want to be able to do this because you cannot sell your business! The business is comprised of people (including you), capital equipment and inventory. You can only sell the *system* that operates your tire business in a manner in which it is successful. It is the value you have added that makes your business worth something. That value is your set of systems. Otherwise, anyone can buy inventory or equipment and start the same business. Why would anyone need to buy it from you?

How about the customer list, you might ask? Does that not have value? Of course it does – assuming you have a *system* of keeping it up to date. In the servicing of automobiles, customer lists are even more valuable than in most businesses. They generally include timed events that allow for genuinely helpful excuses to make contact with a customer. They include history and statistics to which most businesses do not have access.

Plus, if your team truly understands the concept of marketing, you have a list of people you are pretty sure have a very positive disposition toward your business. Virally expanding that list by "personal reference" coupons or other such incentives provides an almost costless method of increasing the value of your asset.

But, as the owner, be careful about being to visible. If you have trained clients that, as the owner, you are personally the key to their happiness and no one else is as good as you, the result is that you have actually *reduced* the value of your business. It is far better to train them to trust your brand and your associates -- not you personally.

On the issue of trust, TIA Executive Vice President, Roy Littlefield, suggests that *distrust* turns out to be an advantage for properly postured tire dealerships. New car dealers seem to suffer from a certain distrust among the public on the pricing of aftermarket parts and services. Tires in particular.

Such distrust is not person-specific. Posturing your brand to be trustworthy does not require your personal presence to be an effective source of revenue.

SYSTEMIZING IMAGE

If your business is good enough to be attractive to someone else, you have done more than simply unlock the door every day. You have created a value by doing *something* that people are willing to pay for. Systematizing that *something* is where you – or any employee – become immaterial to the value of the business. The business has value in and of itself.

But, you say, "I don't really want to sell my business!" In that case, if you have it ready to sell and elect not to, you have essentially bought it yourself. You have the option to sell it or keep it, but at that moment, *it has a value.*

Most people say they don't want to sell their business because, in their hearts, *they know they have nothing to sell!* If you cannot picture the business running without you, the value of your business is limited pretty much to the value of the inventory and equipment -- essentially liquidation value.

IMAGINE TREES AND COWS AND TRACK

Perhaps one of the most valuable images you can have comes from Tom Watson, former CEO of IBM, where he suggests that to get an idea of what your objective is you only need to imagine what your business would look like when it is "finished". When all the parts are in place, it runs as smoothly as any business can run. At that point you are not "doing" or even "managing", but *owning* a "finished" business. For now, your task is to simply work every day toward achieving that image. (Perhaps "simply" is not the best description of the process, but it made for a smooth sentence.

Imagine you own an electric train set. You want to set up a realistic scene to frame the train set. This involves all manner of little railroad crossings, tiny buildings, miniature people and pets, perhaps a mountain or two, cows in the little field, some trestles, cars and trucks, and smoke coming from the steam engine. Add realistic looking grass and trees and you have your own little piece of the world captured on plywood in your basement.

There are thousands of steps to take after the railroad tracks are stapled down. But, you labor on, knowing in your mind, what it will look like when it is "finished". Still, right now, it is a pile of little bags and boxes of parts and a catalog of where you can acquire more pieces and parts.

Your business is exactly like that. You have all the parts or know where you can get them. Now it is a matter of putting it together in such a manner that it does not consume your life, but provides the means for you to have a life independent of the business.

And, just like your business, you know realistically you are never really "finished" because the *Model Railroader* magazine will arrive every month with new little doohickeys you can add to your layout. Nevertheless, standing here today, you can get a mental picture of what the finished layout will look like when you get to the point where you are satisfied. That is the mental exercise to which you are being invited.

Now, if you were not reading, you would be invited to close your eyes. So, read the rest of this chapter and then close your eyes.

DREAM TIME

Imagine what your finished business looks like. How big is it? How many employees? How are they dressed? What does the building look like? What are the colors of the walls? Where do your customers park? What does your car look like parked among them? What are you doing on a daily basis? What new things have you added since you first started imagining this finished project? What are the sales? How are sales generated? What did you see at the last TIA or regional show that you have mentally added to your operation?

In your imaging of this finished business you are totally unencumbered. You do not have employees that are important, but uncooperative. You do not have a lease that runs too long in a location that doesn't quite justify the rent. You do not have accounting records that you have not looked at in weeks because you were too busy *running* the business and not *owning* the business. What freedom!

You may add hundreds of imaging topics to fit your business, but when you do, make notes of what your imagination showed you. This is not a business plan. It might be called a "Dream Plan".

The wonderful thing about this exercise is that there is absolutely no way you can be wrong! There is no risk. No one to tell you it won't work. No commitments to anyone about precisely what you will and will not do. It is your dream limited only by your imagination. Your private plan. Only yours! There are no limits!

It is especially important not to limit your thinking. You are reminded of the quote from Earl Nightingale back in Chapter 6, "We become what we think about most." Limiting your thinking will limit your results. If you think you have a 4,000 square foot shop with three bays, you probably will. If you think in terms of ten 20,000 foot stores with eight bays, perhaps "failure" will hold you to only five. Never considering the possibility of grand scale will hold you to one 4,000 foot store simply because you could not envision anything bigger.

At this point, however, it is important to keep this dream to yourself. Others, who are not in the same place you are, will challenge your dreams, poke holes in your ideas and bring doubts into your process. You do not need those "anti-success forces" right now. Later when you have firmed up your vision, make your Declarative Statement and let them take their shots.

The next concrete steps, of course, are to start writing your dreams down. Use a pencil; keep an eraser handy and use it often. Add to your page with passion and adjust it at a whim. Soon, hopefully, with help from this text, you will gain a great deal of comfort with the business you own – and what it will look like when it is "finished". And, how it feels when you do not have to actually be on the premises to make it work perfectly.

This is the very essence of making the shift from small business thinking to entrepreneurial thinking. It is the only way to stop the *insanity* with which most business owners live day to day. It is The Objective of this text to help you achieve that.

CHAPTER 11

What Do You "Do"?

In some cultures the question is quite rude. In North America, it is very frequently the cocktail conversation starting point, after names and handshakes are exchanged. It is well within the comfort zone for most people. Business owners often take great pride in answering the question, "I own a bakery, hardware store or flower shop." Or, "I am a dentist, chiropractor or CPA." Or, "We manufacture little tiny bolts for GM that keep the cars from falling apart."

True entrepreneurs, on the other hand, often have a bit of a stumble with this question. Some don't even know "what they want to be when they grow up". They might "do" a dozen things simultaneously. To get out of the awkwardness, they will often pick the easiest of their projects for the person asking to understand and offer an answer that, depending on the situation, cuts off further questions – or generates them.

Sometimes the answers are clever to start or they can end conversations quickly. The IRS agent might answer, "I am a fundraiser". Muhammad Ali, back when he was Cassius Clay, answered, "I beat people up."

Those who start businesses who are "Doers" or "Overseers" will be far more comfortable answering the question about what they "do" than will the entrepreneur. The entrepreneur who is totally candid will answer the cocktail question with, "I am a creator" or "I am a dreamer". Even more truthful, but a bit caustic, might be, "I am unemployable". Those cocktail conversationalists who are more comfortable with conventional answers will slowly drift away, but they will have most likely heard the truth, whether they understand the answer or not.

A BETTER ANSWER

It is easy and comfortable to answer the "What do you do?" question with the type of business you own. It is easy to say you own a tire store; it might be fun to identify yourself as a "merchant of safe transportation". If you are technically proficient at the business, you will be relaxed in your self-descriptions.

The relatively few who are entrepreneurs in the tire business, however, put a slightly different twist on their answers. "I own an automotive services business," hopefully being able to add, "with a dozen retail locations in the [your geography] area."

These answers are bigger than the individual. They are telling of a mind-set that says "my business is more than just me". It is an asset of mine. I own it, whether or not I "do" it.

It means that, while I might own a tire store today, I could be in the automotive services business that operates a dozen such locations around the metro area tomorrow.

The point of all of this gets down to mind-set. Doers and Overseers behave and think in ways that are distinctly different from entrepreneurs. There is nothing inherently wrong with either position – unless the individual is thinking one way and behaving another. That is the definition of *Entrepreneurial Insanity*. Doing the same things (production or management) and expecting different results (growth and freedom) can lead to disappointment ("insanity").

WHAT YOU WON'T DO

It is fairly rare, but sometimes the mental limitations of business owners can be chronic. I recently conducted a survey of scrapbook store owners for *Scrapbook Business* magazine. I posed one question about expanding the store to do other services such as photo processing or book printing. One respondent submitted an answer, dripping with indignity, "I am in the scrapbook business. I help my customers produce their crafts. I would never add a service to my store that would harm another business by taking away their customers!" She is not a great candidate for growth – or freedom.

The question gets down to less a question of what you won't do, but what could you do that would grow your enterprise?

LOGICAL GROWTH

Ignoring, for a moment, the harm that will be done to other businesses, the growth-minded tire dealer often has the opportunity to expand with little investment and no significant effort. This can be far easier than opening a second location.

It may be as simple as a strategic relationship with an auto parts store, detail shop, or body shop. You don't have to actually invest in personnel or infrastructure to increase revenues. The key is to be mentally and logistically free enough to search out and cement these relationships. When it gets right down to it, that is the whole point of this book.

Perhaps your employees are asked to closely inspect the insides and outsides of customers' cars as part of their jobs. Offering vinyl-repair or cracked windshield repair services is a natural extension and probably appreciated by customers who learn they do not have to engage a separate service provider.

Sharp-eyed employees will locate the sales opportunities – assuming they don't do the actual selling themselves. Outsourcing larger jobs to upholstery shops and windshield replacement centers expands the opportunity even more. "Spiffing" employees who discover the opportunity has its advantages, too, both in terms of employee satisfaction and assuring the highest number of potential sales.

The point of this example is to demonstrate that any business can be more than it is currently; that growth does not necessarily require investment in equipment or inventory – or new locations.

Growth is the cornerstone of entrepreneurial thinking. Low-cost growth leads to incremental volume. Sometimes judicious investment is added to grow faster. Building systems around this growth allows the entrepreneur the freedom to create even more opportunities.

Chapter 12

How Do You Eat An Elephant?

The answer to the riddle is, of course, "one bite at a time". And, before I go off on a string of stale elephant jokes, let me get to the point I am making. The insurmountable (eating a whole elephant) is quite possible when broken down into the smallest elements of the process (a bite).

Dr. Kenneth Christian wrote a book, *Your Own Worst Enemy: Breaking the Habit of Adult Underachievement* (Reganbooks, HarperCollins) in which he examines the reasons behind why adults do not achieve their full potential. In it, he describes a series of exercises that someone can undertake as the process of achieving a change in personal habits. I have borrowed one of the tasks that, Ken, describes and added some examples to make the point clear.

The process is one of dividing the elephant into bite sized pieces, not just hacking it up, but by breaking it down into logical and increasingly smaller components.

The Goal. This is the elephant. This is the whole thing; the objective of your process. It is the objective that, if simply stated, might seem overwhelming, i.e. "eat an elephant". To avoid the elephant analogy from this point forward, I will suggest a goal that is – or should be – at the heart of every entrepreneur. For our example, the Goal will be, "I want to sell my business." The Goal could just as easily be, "I want to buy out a competitor" or "I want to grow my volume by 400 percent." You get to pick the goal. For our example, we will work on the process of making your business ready to sell.

Wouldn't it be nice if you could simply put a sign out front and wait for people to come by and negotiate with you for the transfer of your business asset? Everyone knows this is generally not going to happen. And so, to be prepared to achieve it, we break the process down into increasingly smaller components.

Step-wise these components include:

THE GOAL >

    PROJECTS >

        TASKS >

            ACTION STEPS >

                ACTIVITIES

Projects. To prepare the business for sale, there are any number of things that might have to be done. In our example, let me suggest a few that might be necessary to prepare a business for sale.

Project 1: Clean and Clear. You have unsold, dead inventory, old promotional materials, returned merchandise and stacks of unread trade magazines. Clearing your business to make it more visually (and psychologically) appealing is a project.

Project 2: Adjust Staffing. You have people you have kept on because, well, they have always been there and they are friends of family friends (or, worse, actual family!). You have energetic contributors to whom you have not delegated enough responsibility. And, you have a couple of holes in staffing you have meant to fill. Project 2 is to clear up all of those things you have been meaning to do staff-wise and have not gotten around to it.

Project 3: Clean up Corporate Records. In closely held companies, when the owner and his or her spouse may hold all of the board seats, corporate decisions rarely take on the importance they do in a publicly traded company. If you are going to get through due-diligence, you will need to clean up those records to show a time-line of decisions made, borrowings approved and officers elected. It is not hard -- as long as you can remember all of the decisions you made in the name of the corporation since your last minutes update.

Project 4: Get Systems in Place. Systems. Those things that make the operation run when you are not there every minute of every day. Systems actually make it possible to sell a business since it is not likely that you can sell yourself or your spouse. If you make lots of critical decisions on a daily basis, replacing yourself with systems will make your business salable.

There could certainly be more than four projects to achieve the *Goal* you have set out, but for this example we will stop at four. The next step is to break the *Projects* down into *Tasks*. For the sake of brevity, we will only look at one Project for our example, but you can imagine the types of Tasks necessary for the others.

Tasks. Breaking Projects down into Tasks makes the process more manageable -- but, not yet "bite sized". Defining the Tasks necessary to accomplish the completion of the Project on the way toward the Goal is the next step. Note: Not all possible tasks will be included. Those listed below are simply examples.

Task 1: Identify all of the areas which need to be system-atized. In a typical tire dealership this might include service writing, advertising and promotions, supply order-ing, coordinating timely deliveries of tires, managing the condition of the waiting areas and other publicly visible space, human resources, safety, bookkeeping and a myriad of other things.

At the management level, you might include systems for decision making, public image and corporate value systems. Task 1 is to define them for your own business.

Task 2: Assess what systems are in place now. Are they written down? Are they being followed flawlessly? Could they be duplicated in another operation in another location and be understandable?

Task 3: Fill the gaps. Where systems are ineffective, they need to be rewritten. Where there are no systems, they need to be written. Where there are systems that are not being followed, they need to be retrained.

Again, there could be many more tasks in this effort, but the above will serve as examples of the process. Next we break the Tasks down into smaller pieces.

Action Steps: These are the easily understood and actionable items that are the foundation of every Goal. These are the pieces that are nicely contained in a single concentrated effort that is measurable and can be confirmed as complete. For our example, we will only work with Task 1.

Step 1: Organization. Purchase a 3-inch ring binder with section tabs.

Step 2: Prepare a format for each system description. This will include the name of the system, the rationale for it, the "rules" to be followed, the measurement process and the manager responsible for it.

Step 3: Consult with those involved in the process to ascertain full information about what is being done, what gaps exist and how the system should be articulated.

Step 4: Write the System Statement in the format described in Step 2.

Step 5: Review the written system statement with responsible staff to determine their understanding of it. Note: They do not necessarily have to agree with it after your explanation of the new system, but they do have to comply with it. It is *your* vision and *your* company. Too much push-back and the subject will come up again when you get to Project 2 (adjusting staffing.)

Step 6: Distribute copies of the new system-based policy to those involved and store a physical copy under the appropriate tab in the binder you established in Step 1. Get each employee to acknowledge receipt of the policy with a signature.

In the above example, the Steps were fairly logical in their sequence. However, in some cases this will not be so clear and this calls for a further division of the "bites" into those you should eat first and those that should come later. You will probably want to rank them from the simplest to the more complex.

Activities. While, in the above example, the Action Steps are fairly discrete, if you have a Step that is more complex, you can go to the fifth level of the breakdown to the Activities level. These are the "bites" we have been working toward.

In the above example, we could break down Step 4 (all of the departments impacted) into the various areas we listed for Systems in Task 1. You could easily write a one-page system for Receiving in a few minutes. If you have more time you could write two or three more.

The point of this approach is that every Goal gets down to the smallest parts. Tackle what you can and eventually you will achieve the Goal. Planning down-to-the-minute "bites", however, is essential to not only making progress, but to eventually accomplishing the Goal.

CHAPTER 13

What Should You Hire You to Do?

Presuming you own a small business now, the question of who owns whom is probably one you have had in one form or another over the time you have been "the boss". Do you own the business or does the business own you?

You may have started the business to gain the freedom of choice of when and where you are working – free from the demands of people who understand less about what you are doing than you do – but, nevertheless, have the prerogative to tell you what to do and when. You ditched all of that so you could do what you want to do.

POWER SHIFT

As the owner, you can do whatever you want. That is until the day when you have the business fully staffed and the scheduled service writer and a mechanic on whom you rely simply cannot make it to work. Now how much freedom do you have?

Or, payroll is coming up on Friday, and a key commercial client has not paid its bill as agreed and, cash is a little short. Whose paycheck does not get cashed – or, sometimes, even written?

Or, the fall family vacation you have planned for months is scheduled for the exact time that a new earlier-than-expected snowstorm hits your area and the mass of customers wanting to convert from summer to winter tires deluges your operation.

In these instances and a hundred more, the business seems to have a bit more power over what your personal preferences might be. If you did not own the business, chances are pretty good you got your day off, your paycheck and your vacation as scheduled.

As the owner of the business, however, you have traded one boss for a host of different ones like bankers, investors, customers, clients, government entities and, even, at times, employees.

Do you know that you could face severe penalties if you were to treat even one employee the way you are treating yourself?

EASY IN; NOT SO EASY OUT

Perhaps you have seen or heard commercials advertising services to help new business people incorporate or form a Limited Liability Corporation. The text of the ad runs something like this, "If you have ever dreamed of owning your own business, get it started right by forming your very own corporation!" They make it sound like getting legally formed is the same as answering the dream.

The logic of this is much like, "If you have ever dreamed of owning a home of your own, we have a hammer to sell you". The distance between a real business and the articles of incorporation are as far apart as owning a hammer and owning a home. It is nonsense.

This is not a discussion of when, if ever, you should take on a different legal form. This is a discussion about what owning your own business really means to you personally. The aforementioned radio ad suggests that getting into your own business is the achievement of your lifelong dream. Any experienced entrepreneur will tell you that the achievement occurs, not when you open the doors, but when you have turned over the keys to the next owner; when you have built, and profitably sold, the business. It is a lot easier to get into the business than it is to get out of the business. But, it is always the goal for the entrepreneur; not always the case with those who see themselves as small business owners.

FINISHING THE JOB

In the last chapter we discussed beginning with the end in mind. Getting a good picture in your mind of what your business looks like when it is "finished". This chapter deals with all of the time in between starting and finishing. All too often the business owner is so totally consumed by starting the business (Doing) or operating the business (Overseeing) that he or she never achieves The Objective of owning a business that provides them their long-sought freedom (entrepreneurism). Millions of lives have been literally crushed by the weight of business ownership. Those who survive are rarely as happy as they pretend to look.

But, it does not have to be that way. By reserving the mental picture of owner rather than operator, freedom can ultimately be achieved. But, probably, more effectively, *without* your constant involvement. Start that plan today!

HOW CAN *I* BE THE PROBLEM? I'M THE *Boss*!

It is unnatural, uncomfortable and counterintuitive. Why should the person who starts the business be the one the business most needs to be rid of? Yet, if you are truly successful as a business owner, there will be a time when you will become the business *owner*, not a key part of the management. As your business matures, you will find that your personal success will grow in opposite proportion to the extent to which your business is dependent on you. Your original objectives of wealth and freedom will start to be achieved. You will be closer to The Objective.

But, it will not happen automatically. It must be planned. The objective of this book, therefore, is to assist you in making that plan.

Part of the problem is that all too often the personality and soul of those who start a business is all tied up in the creation of the business. Their egos are tied up in the idea that they are indispensible to the successful execution of the business strategy they created. It is their source of personal importance. Sometimes these impressions are inherited from Gen One and manifested by Gen Two.

As a consequence, every decision, big or small, must pass through their fingers. All of the key information is kept in their heads; no one can make a decision without checking with them; they can do every job in the place from tire busting to bookkeeping – and, as a result, will tend to meddle in things just to keep that sense of importance.

Of course, along with all of that responsibility comes all of the stress. With no one else in the house competent to make a decision, all of the pressure comes down to the owners. They keep a cell phone – maybe two – near at hand 24 hours per day. They are indispensable and irreplaceable. They never take a sick day; they cannot afford to! That goes for days off or (God forbid!) a vacation, either! More than a few families have been destroyed by such "responsi-ble" behavior.

HIGHEST AND BEST

What is the highest and best use of your time? Assuming, as we did above, that you can do everything, is it wise for you to do so? Assume you can do the ordering, bookkeeping, inventory control, marketing, sales (yes, marketing and sales are different jobs!), hiring and firing, training, opening and closing, pitching in where needed and handling charitable inquiries. Should you?

Doing so will do more harm to a business than if you did none of them. Note: More harm, but not no harm. Someone has to do them and do them correctly. But, the sooner you let go of most or all of them, the more successful your enterprise will be overall. You can't abdicate responsibility, but starting to get rid of as many specific tasks as possible should begin immediately.

Almost always, the owner's main job needs to be to tell "The Story". Another way to put this is to "act out" the company Mission and make sure every employee is so comfortable with "The Story" that every customer understands the Mission without ever having to read it. Here are some examples:

Personnel Management. If your employees know "The Story", they have a chance to place their own behaviors and decisions into a context they understand and can make others understand, too.

Marketing. Your existence in your community or market-place consists of The Story. Marketing is far different from selling. Sure it sets up selling, but marketing The Story postures your enterprise to be understood by your audience.

Sales. If nothing happens until somebody sells something, then nothing gets sold until The Story gets told. You get to write The Story. It makes the business uniquely you – it does not mean you have to act The Story out by yourself.

Bookkeeping. Accuracy of billing statements to customers reflects your company's professionalism. Something as simple as bookkeeping becomes part of The Story, too.

Ownership. Those who have responsibility for telling The Story will have a greater respect for the process if they understand it in the owner's visionary context. It minimizes sloppy work.

RISKING TRUST

Employee IQs seem to double when they are trusted to make decisions. If every little question comes to you for a decision (e.g. "Mrs. Smith says we got grease on her seats, what should we do?" or "The shipment will have to come Two-Day Delivery if we are going to get it on time, what should we do?" or "The local High School wants us to buy an ad in their school play program. What do you want to do?") you will not have time to tell "The Story". If you are caught up in the daily minutiae of making every possible decision, how will you have time to attend Chamber meetings or visit larger commercial clients who do not know The Story yet?

Try a limited risk trust experiment. Pick an arbitrary amount. It could be $20, $50 or $100 depending on your comfort level. Announce to your supervisory employees that any question that can be answered for which the cost of the decision is under $X, they should make it and not ask any questions of you. Any employee dealing with a customer may make a decision to the benefit of the customer when the cost is under $Y.

Your employees are smarter than you think. When they have bought The Story, they will make decisions consistent with that story. They will surprise you.

After a period of time – probably a short period of time – review every decision that has been made involving the expenditure of cash under this policy. Use the review for guidance and redefinition of your dollar risk limits. If the employee is under the cash guidelines you have set, never criticize the decision, rather guide with language like, "Perhaps the next time this comes up, maybe you could…"

Most importantly, add up what it cost you to have the policy. If you have a way of measuring the value of your time, you can make a simple cost/benefit analysis to see if you have made the right decisions or set the right limits.
If being available to answer every little question saves you $50 per day, could you not generate far more than $50 in

profits by doing something else with your time? It is highly likely that loyal employees who understand The Story will make decisions consistent with the right mix of customer service and company profitability. It is very likely that most of the decisions they make will be consistent with yours.

As you gain comfort with the process, you can gradually extend the intervals between the times at which you review their decisions. Periodically, you may want to change the dollar limits. Employees who consistently make poor decisions will need to be weeded out, not because of the dollars so much, as the realization that they do not understand The Story.

Remember, even if you make *all* of the decisions, money will still be spent. The only question is, would significantly *more* money be spent if you let your employees make the decisions themselves?

Not counted in the equation, but clearly beneficial to the bottom line, is increased employee job satisfaction (less turnover), happier customers (they do not have to wait for an employee to "check with my supervisor"), and the aforementioned ability you have to grow your business by being outside of it instead of working inside of it answering low-value questions.

THE RITZ EXPERIENCE

Tom Peters tells about the policy of the Ritz-Carlton hotels in his book, *The Pursuit of WOW!* Any employee at a Ritz-Carlton hotel may make an immediate decision to the benefit of a guest up to $2,000. That means that the waiter who spills red wine on a light colored cocktail dress can buy the dress on the spot. It means that the housekeeper who closes a closet door on a golf club may buy a golf club. Or, it could just mean that the lifeguard at the pool can buy a new popsicle for a child who accidentally drops one on the concrete.

What the owners of the Ritz-Carlton understand is that "things happen". They also understand that their guests already have the ability to pay some of the highest room rates in the hotel industry. They understand that an unhappy event at their properties will be talked about. And, they understand that, if the conversation is about, not the negative incident, but the immediate resolution of the incident, the property and the Ritz-Carlton brand gets a better image out of the experience. Allowing decisions to be made by others in your organization can pay dividends many times their cost.

THE DECISION

There are many steps to removing yourself from your operation. The first is the *decision* to do so. It is the hardest because it is the most counterintuitive. Accomplish *this* objective and you are well on your way to achieving The Objective.

CHAPTER 14

What Does Your Business Look Like Without You?

Everyone pretty much understands *systems*. When you catch a flight you understand the system which has dramatically changed over the past ten years.

You log in online, shop for your destination, best price and right time; buy a ticket with a credit card, the issuer of which will receive a check from you to pay for it. On the appointed day, you will prove, with a government-issued ID, that you are, indeed, the person whose name is on the ticket; and you will check your luggage knowing it has an additional fare to be paid for taking it, that it cannot exceed a certain weight and it cannot be locked with a lock not approved by the TSA. Then, you head for Security where you will remove your jacket and shoes and all metal from your person, pull your computer out of your carry-on, walk through a metal detector and reassemble yourself on the other side. Soon, you will experience the thrill of showing off that "hidden" piercing to an, up-to-that-moment, bored screener. Everybody knows his or her part and, except for the stubborn or stupid, everybody moves through it routinely.

The whole process does not require the airport manager, head of TSA or the airline station manager to be involved. It is a system.

Every element of your business can operate on a system. If you cannot visualize that, you will be limited to owning and operating a small business until you pass it on, burn out on it, or die. Chances are very slim that you can ever sell it for a profit – particularly if you include the salary you would have taken had you spent a similar number of hours employed by someone else, even at minimum wage.

WHY SYSTEMS?

You must have systems because you simply cannot do everything yourself. Even if you delegate and tightly supervise, you cannot manage all the aspects of a business that is growing. There are a certain limited number of things that both interest you, and at which you excel. If anything, those are the things you should be doing. If you are growing your business fast, even those things you love doing will be systematized and performed by others.

Once you are operationally sound with reliable and predictable systems, you will systematize marketing and sales. You will not be able to personally visit with each customer that could do business with you. You will take your special personality and "Story" and convey it to a team of people who will represent your company just as you would yourself. The process is logical and predictable. You only think you are the only one who can tell The Story. It is not true.

One other thing to consider is that you are not invincible. You probably don't take sick days when your employees might. You are willing to "play hurt" to keep the machine moving. But, statistically speaking, at some point you will be pulled to the sidelines. You will have no choice. Whether it is an accident, significant illness or airline strike while you are out of the country, you must plan for the day when you will simply not be able to be there. Statistics suggest that one out of three business owners will experience a loss-of-time incident sometime during their working careers. With adequate systems in place, your business will be just fine when you return.

What you may have to guard against is the feeling of disappointment if it is operating *better* than when you left. Some entrepreneurs simply cannot help themselves and unknowingly slow progress rather than help it by their "protective" presence.

WHAT SYSTEMS?

Sample Tire Inventory System. A Tire Store has a specific product mix that is comprised of various popular tire sizes. In addition there are ancillary items that are routinely used as part of the installation process. The store manager needs to keep enough on hand to keep business flowing smoothly, yet should be able to get stock as needed in a timely fashion. Each item in the storeroom is arranged in the racks or shelves or the adjacent floor in order of manufacturer and size. Every item is listed in corresponding order in an inventory book.

According to Wayne Croswell of WECnology, "There are still many dealers keeping inventory on manual data sheets, in fact, I know of one dealer where they are maintaining inventory in recipe boxes. That's right, recipe boxes!"

When the system was set up, a count of every item in the storeroom was taken and the number was recorded on the respective line in the inventory book – or recipe box. On the day an inventory is taken, any reasonably intelligent person can go into the storeroom and, line-by-line; write down how many of each item there is in the storeroom.

The first column in each line of the inventory book has a "base" number; the number of items of that inventory that should be in stock. Once the count is taken, the actual number is subtracted from the base number and the result is the minimum number of that item that should be ordered from the designated supplier.

Next, the store manager anticipates exceptional needs for the coming week. If there is a special promotion being advertised with a large demand for certain tires over and above the normal stocking pattern, those tires are added to the deficit in the base inventory, or possibly special-ordered if the store does not normally stock them. The combination of regular and special needs comprise the order.

When the orders start arriving from the suppliers, someone is designated as a receiver who will count every item delivered and check it off of the invoice presented. Variances between the order (and what will be invoiced) and what is delivered is immediately noted and confirmed with the delivery person as a shortage.

As the stock is placed in the storeroom, it is placed in the exact manufacturer size order needed to maintain the system as space in the warehouse allows.

The prices for each item in the inventory are taken from the latest invoice and entered into the inventory book (they are always recorded in erasable pencil). At the end of the accounting period, whether weekly or monthly, the number of items in the inventory count is multiplied by the latest price for each item and totaled for a number that represents the number of dollars currently tied up by the inventory based on the last cost method.

While Inventory Management can be done manually, it's a major time consuming process and doing so discourages even taking inventory – and any system that is not used is rendered totally ineffective. With a computerized system, average costing of inventory is much more easily implemented and inventory management in general is much more efficient and accurate.

At the end of the accounting period, the bookkeeper can take the total sales of tires and the total invoices from suppliers and add or subtract the net difference in the inventory. By dividing the cost of tires into the total sales, the owner of the business will know what his cost of goods for tire sales was for the period. Based on this number, management decisions can be made about pricing or inventory stocking levels. It can even offer evidence of theft. A similar calculation can be made for ancillary costs for non-tire items.

SYSTEMATIZE EVERYTHING

Virtually any aspect of every business can be systematized. Think of how many types of businesses are franchised or have multiple locations under one ownership. Assume the business owner can do a set of tasks perfectly. The process is no more challenging than writing down the exact steps to take. All too often, however, there may not even be a system operated by the owner. It could be that each time something is done, it is done on a whim depending on the mood of the individual.

This is a recipe for inconsistency, if not disaster. What happens when someone else has to follow in the leader's footsteps – and there really are none?

Therefore, the process for establishing a business operated by systems would include the following:

- Create a list of absolutely everything that occurs in the life of the business on a daily, weekly or monthly basis. This can be as mundane as the opening procedure. It should be excessively detailed. The opening procedure might include unlocking, turning on lights, retrieving the cash from the safe for the register, checking personnel to make sure everyone has been accounted for and calling replacements, if necessary, and so forth.

- Once the list of activities and processes is complete, look for ways to merge them into categories. The opening procedure could include machine set-ups or calibration procedures, for example.

- Take each process and establish a *stepwise system* for accomplishing it. Too much detail is not possible. Leave nothing to chance. Imagine that the system must run the business and you are totally absent. Imagine that you own 100 such businesses and each must execute precisely the same.

- Next, look for ways to internally generate responsibility. For example, you can establish systems that apply to employee behavior. In the above example about the opening procedure, instead of the opening person having to check on and replace absent employees, the rule could be that an absent employee is responsible for replacing him or herself by calling an off-duty employee to fill in until he or she can get back. If this involves swapping hours (within wage and hour legal limits), leave that up to the people involved. Each employee "owns" the job that must be accomplished. This prevents their problem from becoming yours.

- Write everything down into a multi-chapter *Operations Manual*. Pretend you have never worked in the business yourself and decide whether you would understand your own instructions. Then let a few employees give you an honest assessment, too. [To get help doing this, see page 203.]

- Have someone read a section who has never done the described tasks before. See how he or she reacts to the system and whether the tasks can be executed flawlessly. Obviously, if the task requires technical training before it can be accomplished, you need to have a trained person review your system description.

Perhaps the best example of how this works is McDonald's. This is a business that is based on the assumption of over 200 percent annual turnover and where the team members are generally teenagers. The only possible way for McDonald's to have become a multi-billion dollar company is for the systems to leave nothing to chance. A McDonald's manager's job is less about managing teenagers than overseeing a system to which they have become attuned. The *system* manages the teenagers.

SYSTEMS ARE INVESTMENTS

We have discussed how *systems* create assets. Having systems allows the business to be less dependent on you. The extent to which your presence in the business is insignificant is the distance you have come toward developing an *asset*. You cannot sell a business because you cannot sell people and you cannot sell yourself. You can sell a system.

Further, you can sell a set of systems that you have personally developed to make your business special and successful. These *systems* are your asset. It allows you to use the wonderful expression, "Let me show you how it works!"

In Chapter 22, you will be introduced to an on-line system that will help you develop these types of systems as well as prepare your business for letting you achieve the freedom you seek as an entrepreneur. The program is entitled *27 Weeks to Freedom for Small Business Owners* and is a good next step toward achieving The Objective after you complete this book.

CHAPTER 15

Are You Willing to Get a Little Stingy?

This text so far has focused on lots of ways to posture your business so that it is less dependent on you. You have been relegated to the job of setting the rules (systems) that manage the business so that you do not have to. Topics have ranged from employee policies to marketing strategies. In each chapter, it gets down to how to increase the value of the asset you own.

The most important systems you will put in place, however, deal with cash. When you get right down to it, your business is an asset because it is profitable. The more profitable, the more valuable. It is amazing, then, that so many small business owners do not fully respect the power of cash.

Protecting cash is actually part of your core operating philosophy. You may not make it a public part, but it certainly should be part of The Story you share with employ-ees. How to do so is absolutely part of your *Operations Manual*.

KEEPING AS MUCH AS YOU CAN

Sometimes small business owners can be too good about paying bills themselves. Too good, you ask? Yes.

Without compromising the integrity of your company, pay as slowly as you possibly can. Keeping cash in your pocket is far better than it not being under your control. The longer you can hold onto cash, the less you will need to borrow to operate the business. A consistently lower cost of borrowing will enhance the bottom line. Here are a couple of ideas how:

Do Not Pay Bills Before They Are Due. Surprisingly, many small business people pay bills the day they arrive. Paying early does not enhance your credit rating and is rarely appreciated by those with whom you do business. (Certainly there are exceptions to this observation.) The reason goes beyond just positive cash flow.

If you pay bills early, you "spoil" your supplier. If you ever do have a cash crunch and your pattern of paying early is interrupted, even if you still pay on time at the end of the terms, it will be noticed by the people whom you are paying. You stand the possibility of being judged more harshly than need be if you simply stuck with agreed terms. Certainly pay on time, but never early.

Negotiate Extended Terms. If a supplier appreciates your business, you can ask for extended terms, maybe 60 or even 90 days. The supplier must see some value in doing so, but you may be surprised with the terms you can get just by asking. The terms you get will certainly be no worse than if you had never asked at all.

If you negotiate longer terms, it is essential that this negotiation happen as early as possible in the relationship and absolutely *never* when you are past due.

Lease When You Can. If you are buying depreciable equipment for your business, you can keep such expenditures off of your balance sheet by leasing. You want to make sure that the terms of the lease are not onerous, but if you can get a fair deal, it will dramatically help cash flow, since you generally won't be making down payments or drawing against your borrowing capacity. If you can get the lessor to allow smaller payments with a balloon at the end, all the better, but, of course, you have to plan for the day when the balloon is due.

NOTE: This is a chapter on cash flow. As such, the recommendations are focused solely on that topic. The Buy vs. Lease argument has raged for years. Before electing to lease a piece of equipment, you might do well to consult with your tax advisor or at least listen to alternative funding proposals. Your decision may vary depending on what you are buying, how it depreciates, how much it costs and, of course, the true cost of the money involved.

Controlling the Little Expenses. A nickel here and a dime there. Eventually, they add up to real money. Take the time to micro-analyze every expenditure in your operation. You only have to do this once every so often, so be very thorough. Determine a way that you can measure the cost of every element in your list. This could be from invoices that come in monthly (electricity), or metered usage on office equipment (photocopiers) or inventory fluctuations on consumables (repair supplies). Establish a policy for the preservation of these resources and systems to measure their use. In conveying their importance, you can aggregate the "little stuff" into one or more categories.

Once again, you can demonstrate the compounding effect of small item waste. A stolen box of 97-cent paperclips requires (assuming a 10 percent net) sales of $9.70 to replace them. You can make the point to your team without beating it into the ground. Nevertheless, enforce awareness of the importance of minimizing waste. Make it part of your Story.

CHAPTER 16

Who is Stealing From You?

Sometimes people do not even know they are stealing. When they steal time – yours or theirs – it is cash wasted.

Tim Ferris wrote a book titled *The Four-Hour Work Week* in which he extolled the benefits of time control (not time management) and outsourcing. His point was that in any given day, the average business person gets only about 90 truly productive minutes. It was a shocking thing to read, but, upon reflection, seems about right.

Throughout this text, you have been peppered with ideas about how to create systems that allow your business to run on auto-pilot. In fact, the entire thesis behind Ferris' book was dramatically reducing the amount of time you spend running your business. It is almost exactly the same thesis as *Entrepreneurial Insanity*. The key difference in the philosophies is that in the case of *The Four-Hour Work Week*, the objective is to reduce the amount of work you have to do to make a living. In *Entrepreneurial Insanity*, you are being encouraged to eliminate your importance to the organization so that the business has a greater value. Whatever the objectives, the strategies are very much the same.

STOP THE INTERRUPTIONS

In Chapter 13 we discussed letting employees make decisions up to a certain dollar amount without your approval. Not only do your customers get answers more quickly, your employees gain face and you don't get disturbed. The saved time allows you more time to increase the value of your business. In theory (and practice) it will cost you less for employees to make limited-value mistakes than what you can earn for your business by not dealing with the distraction yourself.

Other ways to avoid interruptions is to stop reading e-mail. Not altogether, but not every time the little "ding" in your e-mail account announces you have a new one. Turn it off! Decide to open e-mails only twice per day. Put an auto-responder message on your e-mail system announcing your new policy and let people who need a more immediate response know they can reach you by your "private cell number in the case of an emergency."

It might require a bit of training to help your colleagues understand the definition of an emergency, but it will eventually pay off. Here is an example of an autoresponder message to accomplish this:

Hello,

In an effort to accomplish more than is normally possible for one person, I have restricted my handling of emails to twice a day – 11:00 AM and 4:00 PM Eastern Time. I will respond to your message at the next opportunity.

If the subject of your email is urgent and requires an immediate response from me, please call my private number at 555-321-4321.

Thank you in advance for your understanding.

Sincerely,
Tom the Tire Man

Similarly, your office voice mail can announce that you will not be picking up messages except for twice per day. The same cell phone emergency procedure can be used to avoid a possible disaster that would be created without your input.

Eventually, you may be able to reduce these tasks to once per day or a couple of times per week. You will learn how few "emergencies" there really are.

GET TO THE POINT

When you are reached by phone, put subtle pressure on your caller to get to his or her point quickly. By answering, "Oh, Hi, Jim. I am right in the middle of something, but tell me what I can do to help you." Jim will get the message, but not feel disrespected.

Such an answer cuts out a lot of chit-chat and still conveys your cheerful willingness to be helpful. At the same time it announces that you are busy and want to get off the phone as quickly as possible. By not allowing Jim to defer and offer to call later, you will get the issue resolved quickly so you can return to productivity.

If encouraged to call back at a later time, Jim may feel the green light to be more comfortable with the chit-chat when he thinks you are not in the middle of something. Further, letting Jim hear the "middle of something" speech two or three times in a row on the same topic may create unwanted tension between you. Get the business done with the fewest number of motions.

SEND A MEMO

If Jim's request turns out to become more than you want to deal with at the moment or to create a face-to-face meeting, ask that he send you a quick e-mail with a summary of the problem and the agenda for the meeting. It is just possible you can resolve Jim's issue by answering his message and avoid the time needed for a meeting or longer phone call, after all.

NEW PATTERNS OF PERSONAL BEHAVIOR

When you start to set up systems and remove your availability from your business, it could lead to the impression that you are not interested. You can avoid that impression by judiciously using your time to simply wander around. Engage in light chat with employees and customers. Pay close attention to what you are seeing. Do not attempt to take corrective action during these tours – particularly if the people with whom you are visiting, and whom you are observing, have a reporting relationship with a manager between you and them.

You will be able to gauge attitude, adherence to established systems and whether the vision of the company is being expressed in the work you observe.

MEASURE EVERYTHING

As your systems are established, much time will be saved if you know exactly what you are looking for. The famous quote from President Ronald Reagan, "Trust, but verify", applies to businesses as well as international politics. In Chapter 19 we will determine the dozen or so key numbers that will tell you what is going on at the end of the period, but it is still important to be seen checking the numbers as they are being accumulated. It all gets down to the psychology of management. Let them know you care. They will increase their caring.

GOOD PRACTICE FOR THE FUTURE

Achieving The Objective will occur when you have diminished your need to spend time in the business to the greatest possible extent. Controlling the time your business and employees pull from you every day is good practice toward ultimately achieving it.

CHAPTER 17

What Do You Do With The Empty Boxes?

The Organization Chart is familiar to every business owner. There are branches describing reporting relationships and responsibilities all leading up to the trunk of the inverted tree to the source of all decisions and wisdom – you.

The challenge for every new and growing business is that there are more branches than bodies. More responsibilities than names to put under them. So they all end up in the same place. Your desk.

As a result, the formal organization chart usually does not even exist in most small businesses. Why draw boxes when they all have your name in them anyway?

Well, there is actually a good answer to that question and that is what this chapter is all about. Yes, you already guessed it. It gets down to *systems* thinking. How do you

159

view your business when it is "finished"? Not, how it is now.

In the early days, the new business owner has lots of hats. Wearing these hats often creates 16-hour days and lots of missed school plays. It is easy to get caught up in the thrill of giving birth to a new enterprise – the answer to the desperate need for freedom! But, in the early days, freedom seems like the light at the end of a very long tunnel.

To assure that the light is not a train coming at you, it is important to visualize the finished product. You are going to be doing many – if not all – of the jobs yourself anyway. Instead of running from task to task, picture a staff of five or six individuals. If there is room, create their work locations. As you go about the various jobs, execute their tasks in different space. If there is not enough room, just use your imagination. So others in your business will not think you are crazy, buy six different color baseball hats and wear the designated color when working on a specific task.

The key is to remember that it is not one giant *job*. It is a series of jobs that will be filled as resources and need dictate. But for today, the organization chart looks a lot like the one you will see when you turn the next page.

It is helpful to draw an organization chart for all of the jobs the business will need, even when you only have three or four employees. It keeps the objective in sight, and the organization of the business in your thoughts as you proceed through the day.

More Than Just Boxes

While the box and line map of your business is helpful, as you are preparing for growth, make sure that each box is "alive" with a purpose and an obligation. For each box, create a document that not only describes the job (the job description), but, also the work product of each job to be done.

When the jobs are more than boxes, it will be good for you to be able to imagine what the job is, what has to be produced by the job and how the success or failure of the job is measured. Then, when you are ready to employ someone else to fill the box, you will have a deep and thorough understanding of exactly what the job entails, whether the candidate seems to fit the responsibilities of the position and how the performance of the individual will be measured in the future. The new employee will, too.

Everybody is in Marketing

As you contemplate filling the boxes and as you are describing the responsibilities for each box, it is important to acknowledge that every box should have a paragraph that clearly states the marketing aspect of the position.

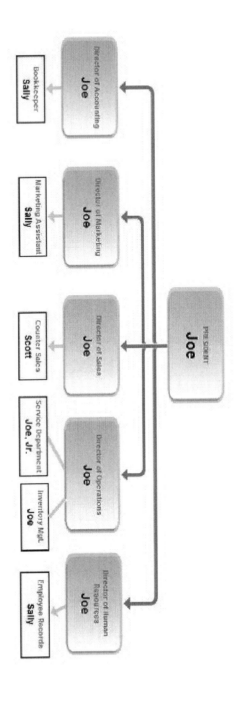

162

If your business is large enough, you may have a Marketing slot other than yourself. The **Marketing** position is reasonably obvious. The job entails positioning the company to be attractive to the greatest number of people who may become interested in doing business with your company.

Similarly, **Sales**, deals the most directly with the customers and will essentially be the "face" of the company to the public. These are service writers internally, or sales reps if they work outside. All too often companies will allow a power struggle to exist between Sales and Service with the customer losing out, no matter who wins the battle. When Service will not support promises made by Sales, the customer loses. When Sales promises beyond the ability of Service to deliver, the customer loses.

Service is very much part of the marketing equation. While the marketing department is responsible for getting a customer in the door, it is Service that keeps them there. Never losing sight that delivery of the tire product or the services requested is a demonstration of the promise made or implied by Marketing, will keep the company focused on its main purpose for existing.

Even **Bookkeeping** is part of the marketing process. When tires and services are purchased they must be billed as agreed. Make certain that your bookkeeping department is not so caught up in "being right" that they lose sight of the larger objectives of the company.

Everybody is on the Marketing Team!

The next chapter deals with the way you can fill your boxes – select your team – in ways that will more quickly move you toward The Objective.

And, it is philosophically opposite of what most business owners do today.

CHAPTER 18

How Do You Pick a Winning Team?

As your business grows and there is the need to fill the boxes, there are many things to keep in mind as you do so. Much of what you need to keep in mind is embodied in the systems you have established and the obligations contained in the position descriptions described in the previous chapter.

As you have developed your business, you have created, in your mind's eye, a living, breathing entity that is exactly the way you want it to be seen in the eyes of the world. It is this entity that will free you from the workaday world. It achieves The Objective of working – so you don't have to.

Every hiring decision you make must reflect that vision in a way that supports it. You must never accept an application from anyone who cannot totally support that vision no matter how desperate you might be for help. Much of your selection process will be with that vision in mind. It becomes the basis against which you compare all of your hiring alternatives.

But, I Already *Have* A Team

Those who are reading this text who have been in business for some time will, undoubtedly, have a staff already in place. This may or may not be a good thing. If you have a team that runs like clockwork and every single person fully understands and buys into your vision, and can help you get to The Objective, then you can skip this chapter.

If, on the other hand, you have uneven performance, non-workplace issues that impact performance or team members that cannot make a decision without checking with you, perhaps you should at least skim this one.

The fact is that owners of businesses that are committed to owning an *asset* often need to make some significant structural changes. More often than not, those who have been comfortable with the business "as it has always been" may not be part of the future of the institution. As difficult as that may be, it is almost always a part of the process.

This chapter will help you get in the frame of mind necessary to judiciously add to your team those people who can help you achieve The Objective. It will also highlight those who will slow your progress. Those must be your "subtractions".

THE TROUBLE WITH
EXPERIENCED MANAGERS

There is a great temptation to hire people with lots of experience to come in and bolster your team. In the interview with such people you will be seduced into the feeling that adding this level of experience will reduce your personal efforts and help your company grow faster. You might even get sold on the idea that you would be foolish not to hire them.

This feeling, however, is the first step toward the abdication of your responsibilities rather than your delegation of them. If the person is as good as he says he is in the interview, there is the great temptation to let him run with things after hiring him – because he *says* he can. And, since he has all of this experience, you can assume that he knows what he is doing. Right?

Sadly, no. Building a business is far more than "getting the job done". Building a business is developing *your vision* of what it should be. Not someone else's. The trouble with hiring "experienced managers" is that they have already been trained in *someone else's* way of thinking. They will start to tell you how to run the company. To allow that is abdication of your role as the head of the company and, very possibly, allowing others to wrest your vision away from you. You must *never* allow that to happen.

Alternatively, it is very possible to locate people who will buy into your vision and who want to become managers on

167

your team. They will, of course, have some innate abilities that include tire service knowledge as well as communication and leadership skills. They will not come into your world wanting to change it. They will absorb your vision and thoroughly understand that it is *your* company, *your* vision and *your* objectives. Agreeing to support what *you* want will get them the job, and the benefits that come with it.

This is possible because you will not be asking managers to manage *people*. They will only manage systems.

You will be asking the new managers in your company to manage the systems you have already developed. The *system* will manage the people. You do not need seasoned managers to try to outguess your systems. Your systems are exhaustively described in your *Operations Manual*. There is no room for reinterpretation there.

But, you might ask, what if you are *not* correct in all of the policies in your manual? Well, you should have a *system* for changing those, too. Here is where people with experience can be helpful. Follow the systems!

OPTIMISM:
THE BANE OF ENTREPRENEURIAL HIRING

Entrepreneurs are inherently optimists. This is a problem. They tend to see the best in people. This occurs particularly in interviews where everyone is putting their best foot forward. Sadly, however, some people are incapable of grasping the vision of someone else and supporting it flawlessly, without trying to "improve" it. Or, they simply reject it altogether. They cannot be motivated or coached. Attempting to force this upon them leads to disappointment and resentment all around.

Guard against seeing candidates as you want them to be rather than what they really are. Having a system (that word again!) for the hiring process can prevent this mistake.

FORGET OWNERSHIP THINKING

One of the more common errors of wishful thinking is to assume you can select people who will "think like owners" of the business. You might have a compensation plan tied to success of the company and assume that it will cause everyone to pull together.

Well forget it! The only people who think like owners are *owners*. It really cannot be any other way. If your employees truly thought like owners, they would not be working for you – they might be trying to hire *you* to manage *their* tire stores! Forever adjust your expectations that anyone will ever think just like you. They can execute for you, and in your vision. They cannot emulate you. They cannot think like you.

THE POWER OF THE WRITTEN WORD

You have been in situations where you are handed a "standard" contract with pages of small print, like buying a car or renting an apartment. You probably don't read it because it is "standard". And, you certainly don't even think about changing a line because it feels (and may be) non-negotiable.

Having a written position description complete with obligations, backed up by a written *Operations Manual* can have the same psychological effect on your new hires. It will significantly deter the idea that your vision is negotiable and that how your company will be operated is subject to any interpretation. Using these written documents in the very first interview will assure that you will not lose control of the interview or the candidate before you can make a decision.

Obviously, significant push-back by the candidate makes your job of selection quite easy. Wish them well. Conversely, you do not want to hire sycophants either. You will be able to spot passive acquiescence a candidate might exhibit just to get the job if you are vigilant.

THE SYSTEM-DRIVEN INTERVIEW

There are thousands of books that offer a step-by-step process for conducting a job interview. These instructions are just fine for a large corporation that has a checklist of government rules they seek to obey and psychographic profiles they wish to match. They employ a system just as you are being encouraged to do and it works for that type of institution.

Yours, however, is a high-growth enterprise. That does not mean you ignore hiring or equal opportunity laws. It means that you are not looking for an automaton. You are looking for an executor; someone who can execute your plan using your *Operations Manual* exactly the way you have it written.

THE HIRING PROCESS VS. A SELECTION SYSTEM

Compare a typical hiring process with one that is a little outside of the box – a *Selection System*. First, let's go over the traditional hiring process that one such book suggests:

1. Review the applicants resume and note any points that need clarification or require more information.

2. Assemble statistics about the company to share with the candidate or to prepare for the candidate's questions.

3. Gain the candidate's confidence by being warm and friendly.

4. Scan the resume for a list of common interests you can discuss before getting into the meat of the interview to make the candidate more at ease.

5. During the interview, let the candidate do 90 percent of the talking. The Interviewer talks more only when describing the job responsibilities to the candidate.

6. Ask open-ended questions, not direct ones, so as to get the candidate to open up more.

7. Ask about work experience in chronological order from his last year in school.

8. Ask about educational experience, not just in terms of technical skills, but to ascertain the candidate's personality, motivation and achievement.

9. Describe the job using the job description. Ask the candidate how he will execute the requirements of the job.

10. Thank the candidate and give him or her some idea of when you will have a decision.

Now, contrast this approach with the **Selection System** process designed specifically to select the candidate that will lead you more quickly to The Objective:

1. Outline the attributes of the ideal candidate for the position for which you are hiring.

2. Review all of the applicants' resumes and select those that exhibit the basic qualities and education to be considered further.

3. Invite all potential candidates to a group meeting at your office or public meeting facility such as a hotel meeting room.

4. In a formal presentation, describe the history of the company, make the Mission come alive with The Story and describe your vision for the future.

5. Answer questions from the assembled group in a manner that confirms the commitment to your vision.

6. Narrow the list of applicants based on their appearance, perceived understanding of the company mission, quality of questions asked, observed interaction with other candidates and physical reaction to the message delivered.

7. After narrowing the field, meet with each remaining candidate individually.

8. Discuss his or her reaction to the description of your vision without reviewing the details. Observe the comprehension of your message in each candidate.

9. Discuss his or her background and experience and how they visualize themselves fitting into the vision as described. Listen for how the candidate fits him or herself into the vision. Be aware of those who want to alter the vision to match their own objectives.

10. Thank the candidate and give him or her some idea of when you will have a decision.

CHECKING REFERENCES

Once you have narrowed your choices down to one or two candidates, it is time for due diligence. You may assume that the references offered by the candidate will be people from whom he or she is pretty sure you will get a positive report. It is, therefore, important in the process of the interview to secure the name of the candidate's supervisors in previous jobs. Just asking the question will provide some information about how the candidate left the last position. You should listen to what the candidate says, but reading between the lines can be useful, too.

Assuming you can get a candidate's previous supervisor to speak with you, given today's litigious environment, be aware that any separation can involve a personal as well as professional agenda. Here, reading between the lines is important, too. Speaking with more than one previous supervisor can give balance to your understanding of the candidate. Asking questions about impressions rather than specific actions may provide better insight. Feelings are sometimes more telling than facts.

DECISION TIME

You have made your decision. Your top candidate did not have any dramatic skeletons in the closet and you are comfortable with his or her ability to understand and commit to the vision. You make the telephone call. The call is carefully scripted to make sure that the candidate enters the workplace exactly the right way. It is consistent with the entire selection process with careful reference to the vision of the company and the new employee's role in executing, not altering, that vision.

Carefully worded and thoughtfully considerate letters are sent to those candidates who are not chosen. Any of them could wind up in your pool again. A lack of consideration of their feelings can only hurt your company's image in the employment marketplace.

THE FIRST DAY

All too often the new employee is brought in on his first day and things become too casual too quickly. The new employee is shown around and introduced to existing staff, probably by nickname. The work areas and equipment are shown off like a visitor getting a tour of the shop.

In many cases a new employee with job experience may get little or no training from the new company with the logic that they were hired because of their experience and should know what to do already. The less formality of this day, the greater likelihood that the new employee will not ever be fully settled and may move on much more quickly than had a more formal process taken place.

The System Approach to the first day is different. It might go something like this:

The first moments of the first day are spent in your office. The vision is reviewed and the systems that deliver that vision are described, perhaps for a second or third time since the interviewing started.

The tour of the facility includes the standard tour and introductions, but the message is not, "Here is how we do things", but, "This is how our systems work". As new systems are described, the way they intertwine is described, as well.

Answers to the new employee's questions are handled in a forthright, not offhanded manner.

Back to your office. Here the *Operations Manual* is delivered and reviewed with the new employee. Questions are answered. The formal statement of job responsibilities is delivered, reviewed and signed. Though the candidate has heard this information during the interview process, this is a formal document requiring a signature signifying an understanding of the responsibilities and their relationship to the systems in place. This is not a job description and it is not an employment contract. It is a philosophical document that is consistent with the message delivered throughout the selection process and becomes the basis for the new person's employment.

Finally, the legally-required government documents are executed for the files and the payroll register.

Do Not Fall in Love

The formality of the Selection System keeps a formal distance and a respect for process. Sometimes, however, employees will come along and embrace the vision so well that they quickly become favored people in the workplace. It is critical for you not to fall in love with them.

First, favoritism will poison a work environment quickly. Second, relying too heavily on an individual who reflects your values so well can have a devastating impact at the time of that person's departure, should it come to pass.

The entire thesis of this book is about building an institution that is independent of any one person – including you. Do *not* fall in love with the individual people.

Love the process.

Do Not Overdo It

Even though in the tire business finding the right people is much more challenging than finding too many, the inherent loneliness of entrepreneurship tends to encourage over-hiring. It is comforting having competent employees milling around. This is particularly true if they are selected as described above and all share a passion for the vision you hold for the institution. To some extent they become a cheering section for the boss and the business. It is infect-ious. And, expensive.

Every new position that is hired needs to withstand the needs test. Does the institution need the headcount to grow? Non-growth expansion of staff is simply additional cost and a drag on achieving The Objective.

CHAPTER 19

If You Aren't There,
Who's Going to Watch the Store?

In previous chapters you should have gotten the point that the value of your business increases as your direct involvement in running it decreases. If, for some reason, you opened the book to this chapter and this is the first thing you are reading, here is a quick explanation: Your business only achieves a value when someone else is willing to buy it for its unique ability to generate a profit that exceeds what he or she will pay you for it. Obviously, you can own a business with value and not have to sell it. But, deciding not to sell it essentially means you are willing to *buy it yourself.* To be valuable to someone else, however, since you cannot sell yourself (or your family or staff), you must develop a machine that is totally independent of all people – especially you.

FLYING IFR

IFR stands for Instrument Flying Regulations. These are
the set of rules that allow a pilot to fly an airplane and be
able to see absolutely nothing beyond the nose of the plane.
It makes flying possible at night, in clouds or heavy fog. It
deals entirely with numbers calculated to tell the pilot what
the status of his airplane is.

The joke among pilots is that IFR-IGL for rookie pilots
means "I Fly Roads – or I Get Lost". This means, of
course, that a new pilot will use known roads or express-
ways as a hint as to where he or she is in the sky. That is
cheating – and, potentially fatal if the pilot ever really
needs to get on the ground in a hurry.

In your case, it means that you have agreed not to meddle
in the business you have systematized, but you sort of just
hang around. That is cheating. It will stunt growth.

Lots of business people attempting to extricate themselves
from the day-to-day operation of their businesses will do
their own version of IFR-IGL. They can't help themselves.

This chapter suggests that you fly your business strictly
IFR. This means that you establish a core set of numbers –
perhaps only eight or ten – that tell you immediately
whether your airplane is sailing along smoothly; whether it
has hit a pocket of rough air; or whether you are going to
fly into a mountain if you do not correct course.

YOUR KEY NUMBERS

In chapter 14 there was an example of an inventory system for a tire shop. Out of the dozen or so steps in the system, a single number emerged that would qualify as a key indicator of the status of the business. That number was the ratio of dollars spent on tires and the number of dollars that were recorded as income. In the tire business the term is "tire gross margin".

You can see that your shop is in much different financial shape if your tire gross margin is 35 percent vs. 20 percent. It does not matter that one tire has a gross margin of 50 percent and another tire has may have a gross margin of 20 percent. It is the average overall tire gross margin that you are looking at.

If your targeted gross margin is 30 percent overall and one period it comes in at 25 percent, this is a signal to look for the source of the problem. If the numbers are within one point or so of your objective, there is probably nothing to do.

If, on the other hand, you are a five or six points away, you should quickly locate the source of the problem. It could be an inventory error, a shift in purchasing patterns by your customers, a significant cost increase in some key tires, or employee theft. In any case, this single two-digit number tells you that your airplane is off course.

Some of these key numbers might include:

- Gross Revenues
- Gross Revenues vs. Forecast
- Gross Revenues vs. Year Earlier
- Gross Profits
- Gross Profits vs. Forecast
- Gross Profits vs. Year Earlier
- Total hours worked per measured period
- Total hours as a percentage of gross revenues
- Car count by day
- Car count by day compared to year earlier
- Dollars per Bay per measured period
- Ratio of sales of tires vs. sales of service
- Ratio of dollars generated by product sales vs. sale of labor dollars (or tires vs. parts vs. labor vs. misc)
- Revenue per Employee
- Revenue per Salesperson
- Revenue per Technician

These key numbers may be different for different operations and different operators will be interested in different numbers, but you should be able to easily determine your own. If you have advisors, they may be able to give you guidance. Better still; compare notes with others in your same business.

As part of this publishing effort, you can register at **www.thetirebusiness.biz** for help meeting non-competitors to compare notes.

If, on the other hand, you are serious about wanting to do in-depth number and idea swapping, contact Norm Gaither of Dealer Strategic Planning who organizes what is called a "20 Group" where groups of tire dealers meet three times a year and spend two and a half days in some serious information exchange. Reach Norm at **Norm@dsp-20group.com** and mention this book when you do.

YOUR TICKET TO FREEDOM

When you have developed your systems and your key numbers, you will have achieved the next major step toward the reason you probably got into business to begin with: Freedom! (The Objective!) By being able to scan a sheet with ten or so numbers on it and know exactly where your business stands, you have the ability to either get back to the operation and start kicking the rear-end of people who should have fixed the problem before you even knew about it, or visit the next commercial prospect, possible strategic partner or tee off on the back nine.

This type of organization also allows you to open additional locations with the same level of comfort. This represents your freedom to grow. This is entrepreneurism.

DON'T TRUST YOUR GUT

Suppose you are a fairly experienced pilot. You have flown in all types of weather and you have a good feel for your airplane. You have good gut instincts about what is happening while you are in the air. No matter how experienced you are, when you are in the middle of a cloud, you could very well be flying sideways, for all your gut can tell you. You *always* rely on the instruments – even if you feel they are wrong!

All too often business people – particularly those with a bit of experience – will claim that they can make gut decisions and things work out right. While that may be true sometimes, there are more than a few such businesses in the entrepreneurs' graveyard. Those with less experience, die sooner.

Even if it does not damage your business, trusting your gut may have the effect of hampering business growth. Your gut may obscure opportunities if you know too much.

Additionally, (harping on the same point again) you cannot sell your gut to someone else. So, let's use numbers.

When it comes time to value your asset, having good, consistent numbers will dramatically increase the value of your business. A prospective buyer can gain comfort from knowing how the company operates and how he or she, with less experience, perhaps, than you, can run the business just fine without you.

DECIDING ON YOUR TARGETS

Many tire dealers claim they are happy with a 50 : 50 mix of tire sales and automotive service. Norm Gaither coaches his followers to aim for what he describes as a more complex 30 : 30 : 30 : 10 ratio scheme. He suggests that tire sales should only represent 30 percent of revenues and that labor and parts should represent 30 percent each with 10 percent being comprised of "Road Hazard Fees" and "Shop Supply Fees".

Following this logic, the service component as defined by most dealers would be in a two-to-one ratio to tire sales. And, since service represents more profit, generally, the entire operation is more profitable. The extra 10 percent almost all falls to the bottom line. Shop supply fees represent an opportunity to recoup costs that otherwise would be considered a cost of doing business and Road Hazard fees (insurance against tire damage) when self-under-written are profitable at the 85 to 95 percent level.

While many in the tire industry survive on a net margin of under 5 percent, almost all of Norm's clients enjoy returns above ten percent. Pricing strategy matters.

"THE RITUAL"

At least, that is how Charlie Creighton of Colony Tire describes it. Charlie says that within hours of the end of the last day of the month he and his managers get a report that details his key numbers and how they compare to the previous month, previous year and the totals year-to-date. Charlie says that each of his managers has 14 days to react to the numbers and make the adjustments that seem appropriate. On the 15th of the month the profit report comes out. This takes the top line numbers, subtracts the expenses and reports net profits. This, Charlie says, "is the important one."

Of course, with 46 stores, Colony Tire is larger than most operations, but the lesson is the same. From the regional managers to the store managers to those who report to them, everyone is aware of the performance of the operation and, if necessary, what needs to be done to adjust. It is a constant monitoring and reporting system.

BUSINESS DEVALUING BEHAVIORS

It is probably more common than not. The owner of a small business isn't taking a salary so he or she simply "borrows" from the cash register for gas or groceries. It becomes a steady flow of tax-free income over time. The legality of this strategy, tax-wise, is not our topic here.

What is our topic is the powerful way in which this reduces the value of a company. In any sale, value is determined by a multiple of something. It could be a multiple of profits or a multiple of gross revenues. For most savvy business buyers, the multiple of gross is much safer. After all, it is very easy to reconcile the amount of money that does not hit the bottom line due to the owner being able to declare a salary of whatever he or she wants (legitimate payroll, not skimming), the company car and other soft expenses that have great latitude in the hands of a closely held business. When these expenses can be tracked, the prospective owner can calculate what the business "really" generates when you (and your car) are not in the picture. This allows the prospective owner to see clearly what money is available for hiring management and for compensating him for his investment.

If it is agreed that a fair price for the business is 1.5-times gross revenues then a company selling $1,000,000 per year would sell for $1,500,000. (NOTE: This should not be any indication of what a normal sale arrangement would be in the tire business. The ratio could be virtually any number based on the industry and business history. The numbers used here are simply to make a point about skimming.)

For every $1,000 dollars that you borrow from the company cashbox, it reduces the value of your business (in this example) by $1,500.

It will do you no good to wink at the buyer and say, "Well, the sales are actually higher, but (wink!) you know how things work in a small business. We really grossed about $75,000 more than what you see on the books." That almost never works.

Your safest route toward building a valuable, saleable business is to treat it like an IRS auditor were sitting on your shoulder every minute of every day. It can be far better for you to take a salary even though employment taxes will take a bite out of you twice, once personally and once for the business, if you can demonstrate total fiscal clarity for your enterprise.

If you have clean books, your value can be fairly and quickly established by a sophisticated buyer. If the books look soft, your prospective buyer will sense that and discount an offer even more to cover the fuzzy things he can't see in your books. Even if you never plan on selling your business, having a clean set of books is the best way to keep your options open. You never know what the next day might bring.

CHAPTER 20

Where is the
Marketing Department?

In Chapter 17 we talked about how every part of your business from sales, to warehousing, to shipping to accounting is really part of the marketing process. Virtually every function touches the customer in some way. To allow any employee or supervisor to operate without an acute awareness of that fact is severe mismanagement on your part.

Marketing is all about image. And, growth is all about marketing. And, everyone on your team is responsible for marketing. The Marketing Department is *everywhere*.

"GOOD AFTERNOON!"
You see evidence of companies that understand that. Go to a top quality tire shop and walk near a mechanic. Chances are very good that you will get a smile and a greeting. Is this guy on the sales team? The answer is probably no. Is he on the marketing team? Absolutely. Does he know it? Absolutely!

Contrast that with the last time you went to the post office or service department of your cellular provider. While there are notable positive exceptions, you have experienced those occasions where you were made to feel that your business was an interruption of their day, not the reason they are there to begin with.

Possibly this is because it is hard to find a competing letter delivery system and you are stuck in a two-year contract with your cell provider anyway. But, this should never matter. Not, at least, in the company you are building. *Everybody* is on the Marketing Team.

THE 5-SECOND APPRAISAL

Remember an occasion where you walked into an establishment for the very first time. What did you see? Chances are you did not see anything; rather you felt it. Impressions are made without conscious thinking.

If you moved to a conscious assessment, and you saw hand-scrawled signs, dirty carpeting, unclean windows and a receptionist chewing gum like no tomorrow, you got more than an impression, you got an assessment. If you were going to this establishment to find a specific part for a machine that is broken and this was the only place for 50 miles that has it, neither your impression nor your assessment may matter. You buy the part and leave.

Alternatively, if you walked in and the signage was professionally produced, the public areas are spotless and the receptionist is dressed in a company shirt with a nametag, you got a different impression. It might not make much difference in where you bought the part, but it certainly would deliver a different image of the company with which you are doing business.

If you were invited back to the warehouse you would likely see rows of immaculately kept and labeled inventory. It is why you were serviced in under three minutes whereas, in the earlier scenario you might have stood around for fifteen minutes – not necessarily because they could not find your part, but because the parts clerk was on break and was outside smoking.

When you enter a business for the first time, you get an immediate impression. In five seconds you know a significant amount about the business, the owner, the people who work there and you make a mental assumption about the quality of the product you will receive from the transaction. Possibly, the better the place looks, the less price sensitive you become.

And, all of this happens without you even thinking about it. It is totally unconscious. You did not enter the establishment to conduct some sort of inspection. You came to buy something. Maybe. If the unconscious moves into the conscious, you might decide not to – or you might even decide you could become a life-long customer right at that moment. It is a powerful moment in time. It is that first impression. It can only happen once.

Now apply that knowledge to your own business. How does your business look? Not to you; to someone looking at it for the first time. How are your employees dressed? What is the impression you get when you spend five seconds looking inside your front door, your service bays, your showroom and your customer waiting area?

SEE IT WITH NEW EYES

One way to get a clear picture of your customers' first impression would be to take a video camera and walk in your front door. Scan right and left. Zoom in on items that might catch a customer's eye. Is it broken linoleum or a faded old sign or a photo hanging crooked or a left over coffee cup? Do not worry about what you are filming, just keep shooting. Allow yourself to go wherever a customer might go or see. The restroom, the service writers desk, the waiting area or the garage area. Film both high and low. Notice the displays, the floor, the surface areas, the corners, the parking lot.

While you are doing this, take a note of "negative signs". You have seen them in many businesses, "No Checks", "Customers Not Permitted", "No Claim Check, No Laundry!", "No Shirt, No Shoes No Service". Little nagging bits of terse communication to let the customer know who is boss. Do you have any of these? Do you think there would be a more friendly way to "maintain control"?

Now in the quiet of your office, play the tape back. Imagine you are seeing your business for the first time. There is something about watching it on a screen that is far more focused than looking at it in person. Take a pad and make notes of what you would notice if it were someone else's business. What impression would you get?

The results of your examination can all be filtered into one system or another. Things are the way they are, not because you do not care; it is that it is easy to become blind to things you see every day.

HOW SYSTEMS COME INTO PLAY

It is your restroom and you use it all the time in an automatic fashion. You don't see the bar of soap with residual dirt on it. You really had not noticed that the toilet paper holder was crooked due to a missing screw. The device that makes the air fresh ran out two months ago and you have been meaning to replace it, but you have been busy. It does not get done. What kind of a system could fix these things?

You have probably seen it dozens of times. Maybe you did not pay any attention. On the back of the restroom door is a one-day calendar with the hours broken into 30 minute segments. In each time segment prior to your visit, there is an initial in the box next to the time block.

Someone is assigned to go into the restroom and check for a specific number of things such as adequate toilet paper, flushed toilets, clean floors, dry sink areas and adequate paper towels. The owner of the business in which this restroom resides never even remotely thinks about these things. That is because there is a system. And, the signature in that little box on the sheet on the inside of the door assigns accountability to the activity.

Now, your business probably does not need 30-minute restroom inspections as a restaurant might, but how about twice a day? Who should be responsible for it? It does not really matter as long as someone is. And, knows it.

The point is, a *system* that made it someone's responsibility means you personally will never have to think about a dirty sink, broken toilet paper holder or whether the air freshener is empty ever again. A *system* would make sure a refill air freshener was always in stock. Fresh soap, too.

EMPLOYEE "RIGHTS"

Realize that this text is written to the owner of a business. Understand that the next statement will surprise some people. Others will understand it immediately.

Your employees have no rights. They do not have the right to "be themselves". They do not have the right to "dress for comfort". They do not have the freedom to gross out a percentage of your customers because they have elected to pierce parts of their face with metal decorations. Their "rights" cannot be in conflict with your marketing model; your image; *your vision*.

If your model, image and vision can accommodate a more relaxed appearance portrayed by your employees, fine. But, it is always *your* decision, not theirs. All too often employers get caught up in the notion that they must be open minded about young people. That is absolutely not true.

As you begin to remove the insanity from your business, you may remove people who will not conform to your new image. An Indianapolis-based restaurant called Steak-n-Shake has its policy in neon across the wall next to the kitchen. *"In Sight, It Must Be Right"*. No one, whether customer or employee, can escape that bright red neon fact. Steak-n-Shake meant that for food, facilities and employees alike. The food is standardized, the facilities are impeccable and the employees are dressed in uniforms that match their jobs. None of them look like customers. And, by the way, there is a checklist on the back of the restroom door proving that they are checked every half hour, and by whom!

If your employees are visible to the customer, they dress the way *you* want them to look. If they cannot remove their piercings before work so there is no evidence that they exist, you have no obligation to hire or keep them. (There was actually a situation where the candidate got through the interview process before putting the ring back in his eyebrow and the employer felt powerless to do anything about it.)

Think about the day when your business is finally for sale. What will the prospective owner think when he reviews your team? For example, does he see a group of employees in clean company logoed shirts or a hodge-podge of randomly selected, "comfortably dressed" people. Every day between this one and that, your customers will be making the same observation.

The point? You developed the vision. You are the boss. *Do your job!*

THE CUSTOMER IS (NOT) ALWAYS RIGHT

The common saw that "the customer is always right" has the feel of a nice simple system, doesn't it? If the customer is always right, then the person representing the business in the transaction simply caves into whatever the customer wants. Nice, clean, simple – and, wrong!

Customers are *sometimes* right. Regardless, it is the job of the person representing the company to make the customer *feel* right in any case. Usually, that is all it takes. From there, some fair resolution can be met. Letting the customer run roughshod over the situation can be expensive and debilitating to the morale of your staff. After all, the *company* is not wrong even though someone in your company might have been wrong.

This is where we get back to marketing. A comfortable resolution to a disagreement not only keeps the customer, but has the tendency to spread goodwill. In the example earlier of the Ritz-Carlton approach to resolving issues in favor of the customer, the management knows people will talk more about a happy resolution than if nothing negative occurred at all. Treated properly, the customer will tend to empathize, cooperate and admire the company for its corporate attitude.

Allowing your employees to have the latitude to make decisions on the spot to resolve issues without "checking with my manager" can be very powerful. Teaching employees how to diffuse a disagreement without giving away the store, makes them even more responsible for the results.

NICHE MARKETING

A niche is generally a small part of the market on which a business focuses to gain an advantage in sales. Mathematically, it does not seem like what you think of as a "niche", but it is an odd mindset when you think of women as a "niche".

It is odd because, according to Jody DeVere of Ask Patty fame (**www.askpatty.com**), women comprise over 60 percent of all tire purchases. How could this be a "niche" by any reasonable definition?

The distinction is almost parallel to the confusion between a small business owner and an entrepreneur. It is what we assume, not what really is.

We think of small business owners as "entrepreneurs" because the term is misused. By now, I hope we have dis-abused you of that thinking. We think of tire purchasers as being men because of historical roles in keeping the family car on the mend and ready for service. Any historical depiction of a tire store, would have to include a scantily clad woman on the shop calendar *Men* go here, it screams. Women can't be offended by such a calendar, because women simply would not be there to see it. "Just us guys."

Such assumptions die slowly, as Jody can attest. Her "Ask Patty" training programs make it abundantly clear where the bread is buttered when it comes to most tire purchases. Those who ignore this do so at their own peril. In fact, you can even obtain a "Female Friendly" certification once you have learned all of the communication and marketing strategies that Jody teaches.

The point to be made is, marketing is very much like pointing a gun. You must know who your target is so you can craft the message. Crafting a message to women is a decision, just as much as focusing on the off-road tire segment. And, (hint) there are more women.

STRATEGIC RELATIONSHIP MARKETING

No discussion of marketing would be complete without discussing strategic relationships. With millions of businesses selling billions of items, it would be impossible not to find synergy right in your own back yard. Perhaps the least expensive path to growth in sales is to cooperate with people who are selling to the same clientele, in the automobile service business, that can be as obvious as a gas station (that no longer provides service), towing companies (that do not service tires), body shops, auto parts stores or tire shops that carry SKUs that you don't (or vice versa).

Less obvious, but equally important, are barbers and beauticians who have lots of time to listen (and make suggestions), golf shops where conversations range widely, bars where bartenders get to listen, too (and make suggestions), or high school auto shop teachers who can direct current and future purchases – and maybe provide interns for your business.

Perhaps you will even find a strategic relationship in working with various women's groups. Jody DeVere would have us believe so.

Taking a good look around can lead to cross-selling or mutual-benefit arrangements where both parties gain from the relationship. It is important, however, that your selected partners match up to the image you are trying to convey in your marketing efforts. Poor partnering selections can do more damage than good.

MARKETING REDEFINED

Most marketing books deal with the mechanics of marketing. The four "P's" (Product, Place, Promotion and Price). In this text we invite you to deal with marketing on a more cerebral level. View your company through the eyes of your customer (and ultimately the eyes of the prospective buyer of your company). You can nail down the mechanics of marketing and push as hard as you can. Without an intuitive look at how the market sees you, however, the effort may fall short of helping you achieve The Objective.

Everything is marketing. And, *everyone* is responsible.

CHAPTER 21

So, What Will You Do With All This Free Time?

Your mastery over *Entrepreneurial Insanity* occurs when you can stand back and watch it work. When you are invisible, but present, for your staff. When you have gotten past describing what your business does and moved to where you can show off how it works.

As this book concludes, perhaps you have just begun. And, when you accomplish the task of removing yourself from the center of the action, you will have begun again. But, this time you will have truly begun your life as an entrepreneur, leaving the mantle of small business owner behind.

At this point you get to be like the fly-on-the-wall. Almost invisible, but present. You get to watch what is happening through the tiny peephole of a dozen numbers electronically delivered to your telephone wherever you are in the world. You will know at a glance that your airplane is flying accurately and smoothly. So, what will you do with all of this free time?

Will you grow the business through sales in a way that only the owner can? Will you examine weaker (or stronger) competitors with the possibility of acquiring them to increase your size and market share? Will you take the systems you developed and open an entirely new, but parallel business in another location? Any of these activities can grow your wealth based on the security you have gained by establishing systems that replaced you as the key ingredient.

Will you engage those business owners mentioned in the previous chapter?

Will you take your spouse on that long vacation you have promised since the day you opened the doors? Will you write trade magazine articles instead of just reading them -- that is, when you had time? Will you volunteer in your community, both as a way to give back and as a way to be exposed to those who will want to do business with you?

Perhaps you will travel in circles where you can drop the seeds that result in people knowing that, under the right circumstances, your business is "in play" and could be purchased at the right price. Once you have developed your plan and followed it, you will enjoy all of the freedom that you deserve.

But, realize that by accomplishing The Objective, you have moved forever from small business owner to *Entrepreneur*.

CHAPTER 22

I Understand It,
But What Do I DO?

From speaking engagements and magazine articles I have had readers contact me and ask the question above. It was not that they did not understand the theory; it was putting it into play that was concerning them. Often they were too busy to achieve the freedom they sought.

That is when I decided to create a sort of "personal trainer" system that will help small business owners become entrepreneurs. You are invited to consider the program:

27 Weeks to Freedom for Small Business Owners

In this interactive program, you will be taken through a series of steps that can lead to your freedom from working in your business as a key player to having your business work for you as the owner of a valuable asset in about six months. The program includes weekly video instructions with links to resources and forms that make your task not only possible, but easy. In addition, you receive a quality binder with subject tabs that will serve as your company *Operations Manual*, otherwise known as "your ticket to freedom".

Own a business that is a true asset. Move from being a small business owner to being an entrepreneur. Leave the insanity behind.

Please visit:

www.27WeeksToFreedom.com

Note: Since this program was first announced, some business owners insisted that six months was too long for them. They wanted to be "fixed" *now*! To accommodate them, a time-condensed version of the **27 Weeks** program has been developed. Same materials and steps, but much more "hands-on" help from the faculty. You can still go to **www.27WeeksToFreedom.com** for information and see the 9-Week option. Both programs culminate in a live 3-day conclusion and graduation in Las Vegas.

AFTERWARD

WANT MORE?

If you have found this book to be thought-provoking and you would like to keep up with new ideas along the freedom-for-owners line, you are invited to go to **www.thetirebusiness.biz** and register.

You will receive new ideas every few days and will be invited to join other business owners in groups, in non-competitive markets, conducted over VoIP bridge telephone lines.

Keep up with the latest ideas and be in a position to form some great strategic relationships.

www.thetirebusiness.biz

INDEX

10250380R0

Made in the USA
Lexington, KY
07 July 2011